Manifesting Your Heart's Desire

Fred Fengler
and
Todd Varnum

Published by HeartLight Publishing
143 Weed Road
Essex Jct. VT 05452-2725

ISBN 0-9641305-0-5

Printed in the United States of America

Contents

Acknowledgments

We would like to thank all the people who contributed their life experiences to this book. Faithfully keeping daily diaries, recording manifestation experiences on auto tapes and attending monthly group meetings required a high level of dedication and commitment coupled with a constant willingness to enter unfamiliar territory. Participants in the manifestation project were requested to not only search their own souls for their true heart-felt dreams and desires, but then to openly share these revelations with others. The result of this on-going sharing was a contagious quality of inspiration, support and learning.

Without the enthusiasm, courage and willingness of many contributors to stretch beyond and play with often cherished personal beliefs, this book would not have been written.

CHAPTER 1

Mind over Matter

Though Frank used his garage only to store wood and gardening tools, the leaks in the roof annoyed him. It was spring, and Frank decided to have new shingles put on that summer. He didn't care when it was done so long as it wasn't too expensive. He often imagined how the new roof would look, but he took no further action except to chat with a neighbor about the needed work.

About a month after he decided to have the roof repaired, there was a knock on his door. A roofer who had been working in the neighborhood had heard that Frank wanted to have some work done. The roofer said he would be willing to do it for around $1,000 and could start in two weeks.

I remember thanking him and taking his business card, but I felt cautious about making a commitment. Something did not feel right. One thousand dollars was a lot of money. Anyhow, there wasn't any rush. It was still early in the summer. I felt quite relaxed and confident about the job being finished over the summer.

A week later came another knock on the door. It was a local carpenter who had been laid off. He was going from house to house seeking fix-it jobs. Frank showed him the garage roof. His estimate to repair it was $500, including materials, and he could begin the next day. Frank told him to go ahead.

The job was completed within three days. The quality of workmanship was excellent.

In the fifteen years he had lived in his home, no roofers or carpenters had ever come to Frank's door. Nor did any come in the three years following the repair--with one exception. That same summer Frank's back porch needed a new set of wooden steps. The old ones were rotting and becoming dangerous. Within a few weeks, a different laid-off carpenter came to his door asking for work and the process was repeated.

Tom needed to find a consultant. His friends recommended a man whose qualifications seemed perfect, xcept that he was living somewhere in California, 3000 miles away. Tom had heard he occasionally came to town and stayed with a friend. It became increasingly clear that he should meet this consultant.

It didn't take a moment and I had this clear intention. It was not that I wanted to meet him but that I was going to meet him. I had no concept of how this would happen. . . . I had created a space and knew it was going to happen. I had this desire to meet him and I allowed it to happen. I trusted and let it go. I also had a strong intuitive knowing.

It was Thursday. The following Monday, at a class Tom was attending, he was approached by a woman he had never met. She began telling him about an interesting man she had met the night before who had just come to town from California. She added, "I don't know why I am telling you this." Tom realized she might be talking about the consultant.

"Is his name Tony Kesnovich?" he asked.

She looked surprised. "Yes. How did you know?"

Tom replied, "Oh, I've heard about Tony. I've been wanting to connect with him."

She gave him the consultant's local phone number. Tom arranged a meeting with him for the following Friday. Later Tom found out that Tony had been in town for only a few days.

The whole process, from his voicing the desire for a consultant to their first meeting, took one week.

Dot had always loved a certain kind of Russian doll that represented the theme of the Wizard of Oz. She had planned to buy one locally, but the store had changed hands and no longer carried it. She had no idea how to find the doll she wanted. "I always had it in the back of my mind to get one for myself and one for my niece, who also has a doll's collection."

Two years later, she was window shopping in a neighboring state. A companion grabbed her sleeve and pointed out the doll to her. The shopkeeper told her that she had received only two of these dolls, and they had arrived at the store just two days earlier. The shopkeeper had brought them on a whim. With much joy, Dot bought both, intending to give the second doll to her niece.

When Sarah learned that the evening's cabaret performance was sold out, she was upset. She had so much looked forward to it. Even the waiting list was long, she was told; she should not count on a cancellation.

When she got home that evening, a message on her answering machine told her there <u>had</u> been a cancellation--but they had been unable to reach her. The ticket had gone to someone else.

Somehow Sarah knew she was meant to see that show. Though disappointed she had missed the phone message, she met a friend at the door to see if there were any "no shows." At first the hostess said "no," but Sarah asked her to check again. The hostess walked around the room looking at the seating capacity for all the tables. When she returned, she told them that she had found two unfilled seats at the head table, directly in front of the performance. As Sarah described them they were the "best seats in the house!"

Reflecting on her state of mind on the day of the performance Sarah replied that she just knew she would see the show.

> I believe that consistent desire, unfailing trust regardless of external appearances, and perseverance are key factors in manifesting our goals. I just didn't give up, I kept the desire alive. But I was not burdened with the obsession that it had to happen. I just knew that if it was right it would.

Coincidence or Creation?

Did these four people actually create the circumstances that resulted in the realization of their desires? Was it just coincidence that Frank was home to answer the door when the roof repairman happened to come by? How did he "know" to wait for the second repairman? Why was the roof repairman looking for work just when his services were needed? And how did he know which blocks or homes in a city of 40,000 to approach for jobs?

One might argue that over the course of two years Dot might just happen to find a store selling such a specialized doll. Yet Dot could not believe her good fortune to have arrived at that store two days after they had arrived. Had she visited three days earlier, they would not have been there. Had she come later, some one else might have bought them. She also happened to have a friend who noticed them. And how coincidental that the shopkeeper had ordered two of these very unusual dolls and that both were still available.

Tom also believed that he would connect with the consultant, without knowing consciously how he would do so. Sarah had no doubt that she would get in to see her concert, even though external events could have discouraged her. She instead trusted some internal state of consciousness.

Each of these people had no doubt that they created the experience or object of their desire--although none of them could explain how they were able to do so. Tom could not have known that he would meet a stranger at a class who would share the information he needed to locate the consultant. What motivated her to talk to him, especially about an incident that had nothing to do with the class? Frank had no idea ahead of time how his roof would be fixed. Dot might have found the dolls advertised in a mail order catalogue. Sarah might have gotten her reservation by a phone call. All were open to a variety of means of achieving their goals. They kept the end in mind and did not worry about how their goal would be realized. At some point a trusting "leap of faith" occurred for each of them.

In his book <u>Synchronicity:The Bridge Between Matter and Mind</u>, David Peat refers to the concept of "synchronicity" as events that defy "our appeal to a 'scientific' view of nature." The essence of a synchronicity is one's certainty that so-called coincidental events are personally meaningful. An outsider could probably explain all these events in terms of scientific probability or causality. But the person who experiences the events has little doubt of a connection. Whether the person actually created the connection or sees some divine pattern in which he or she is a participant depends on the belief system of the individual. What was certain for each of the four persons discussed was that the events, at least for them, were meaningfully linked.

Do Our Beliefs Create our Experiences?

Every summer Tim went sailing for two weeks on his vacation. And it seemed that every year the weather was miserable, no matter what two weeks he chose. One summer he invited a friend to share the second week of his vacation. Just as he knew it would, it rained off and on most of that first week. To make matters worse, there was little wind for sailing.

At the beginning of the second week, as his friend arrived on board, the weather cleared and the wind picked up. Tim was absolutely amazed. The first words out of his mouth to his friend were, "Boy, are you lucky!" His friend turned to him calmly. "I always have good weather on my vacation," he said, as if it were no big deal.

How could this be? Was Tim always unlucky and his friend always lucky? Could his friend control the weather? Tim remembered how his parents always seemed to experience bad weather also. He still remembered his father saying, "Wouldn't you know that these are the two days of vacation I have all year and it rains." Even when his family did experience some good weather, he remembers his father complaining about the days with the bad weather.

Tim suddenly realized there was nothing extraordinary about his friend's ability to always have good weather. Both he and his friend were equally powerful in obtaining what they expected. They were just creating different kinds of weather. Tim expected bad weather and was "rewarded" for his belief with rain and heat, just as his friend who "always got good weather" was rewarded with sunshine and pleasant temperatures. In that moment, Tim realized that this was not a given but a choice.

This realization allowed Tim to change his beliefs and expectations about the weather. From that moment on, he also enjoyed sunny weather on his vacations. His parents, not having this realization, continued to tolerate unpleasant weather on their vacations. Tim noted that he and his parents were equally powerful in realizing their expectations. The outward manifestation of weather conditions in their environment clearly conformed to their beliefs and expectations. When the expectation changed, as it did for Tim, the outward form of the weather also changed.

Visualization in Athletics

As Paul turned fifty, he realized he had to change his tennis game. No longer did he seem to have the power of his younger days. Worse still, he had developed an annoying discomfort called "tennis elbow" whenever he played. It was so painful at times that for days after he played he could not pick up an object without feeling pain in his right arm. He did not want to be dependent on cortisone shots, as one doctor recommended. He was considering giving up the game. He decided he had to develop new tactics and skills to reduce the tendon flareup in his elbow.

About the time these thoughts were taking shape, his sons gave him two books they felt would help. The first was The Inner Game of Tennis by W. Timothy Gallwey. The second was Tennis: The Mind Game. Both books stressed the power of values and belief systems and how they affect performance. His emotional state and his ability to move beyond thought, analysis, and self-judgment, he learned, were crucial components in improving his game. Visualization techniques and exercises where he mentally "rehearsed" himself during peak performance periods would prepare him for actual play.

Paul also began to read about experiments where mind was a critical component in enhancing athletic skills. One study involved basketball players who wanted to improve their foul-shooting ability. Three groups of equally able players took part in the experiment. The first group shot free throws for twenty minutes a day for six weeks. The second group visualized themselves shooting free throws perfectly for the same amount of time. The third group neither visualized nor practiced. After six weeks, the group that practiced shooting had improved 24 percent. The group that visualized shooting free throws improved 23 percent. The non-practicing, non-visualizing group did not improve. In other words, the players who visually "rehearsed"--who practiced only in their minds-- did almost as well as those who physically practiced on the courts.

Similar experiments have been done with dart players. And soviet researchers studying world-class soviet athletes found that combining practice and visualization was particularly successful--especially when the mix favored the mental exercises over the actual practices (say 75 percent to 25 percent). The major reason "such relaxed visualizations have such a powerful influence on our lives," suggest the basketball researchers, "is that the body doesn't know the difference between what is real and what is imagined."

Reading these accounts helped Paul to change his own belief about the inevitability of his condition. If the body could be led to think it had practiced a particular skill, perhaps it could also be taught to heal itself.

Mind Power in Medicine

Carl, a university professor, felt a sharp stab of pain as he stepped off the speaker's dais. He had twisted his left ankle, which became swollen and painful as the afternoon progressed. He barely hobbled home that evening and sank into his easy chair, preparing himself for more pain and stiffness the following day.

I thought of ice and heating pads but then decided I would use my newly acquired visualization tools to bring down the swelling. Every half hour or so that evening, I visualized myself climbing my stairs to bed in comfort. I also saw my ankle's swelling decreasing. By the time I went to bed, there was minimal discomfort. And the next morning there was only the hint of any discomfort. Perhaps a complete "cure" would have overtaxed my belief system of my own ability to heal myself. Of course, it might have healed anyway. I had twisted ankles before and none had ever healed this rapidly. But perhaps I did not damage it as much this time as I thought. Perhaps if I had twisted my other ankle I could have used it as a control. And so goes the mind of a scientist.

Of course Carl's personal experiment did not have the control and sample size that other researchers have used in studying the healing properties of the mind over the body.

Placebos have long been noted for their effectiveness in curing disease or disability. In one study, patients who had been hospitalized with bleeding ulcers improved markedly compared with a control group when the doctor assured them that an injection of distilled water was a new medicine that would cure them.

In another study, patients at San Francisco General Hospital were assigned to either a group prayed for by home prayer groups or to a group not remembered in prayer. It was a random double-blind study in which neither patients, nurses, or doctors knew which group the patients were in. Prayer groups were given names and asked to pray each day for an unknown specific patient. The results? The prayed-for patients were one-fifth as likely to require antibiotics, and less likely to develop complications or die. In his evaluation of this experiment, Larry Dossey comments, "If the technique being studied had been a new drug or surgical procedure instead of prayer, it would have been heralded as some sort of breakthrough."

In his popular book Quantum Healing, Deepak Chopra, a practicing endocrinologist, reports on several studies as well as many of his own cases of patients who had "spontaneous remissions" of cancer. He reports that the patients' attitudes about their illnesses changed prior to the remission. They found some way to become hopeful or courageous, often despite their physicians' pronouncement of hopelessness. In contrast, people in a "climate of negativity" have greatly reduced abilities to heal. "Research on spontaneous cures of cancer conducted both in the United States and Japan has shown that just before the cure appears, almost every patient experiences a dramatic shift in awareness. He knows that he will be healed, and he feels that the force responsible is <u>inside</u> himself but not limited to him." Chopra concludes, "Your body is the physical picture in 3-D of what you are thinking."

<u>Developing Your Awareness of Your Power to Create</u>

When Tom experienced bad weather, he could have called it "bad luck" or fate, or perhaps even blamed the weatherman. But Tom decided to change this pattern through a transformation in the way he perceived himself and his experience. Carl decided to focus on "seeing" his swollen ankle healing quickly. Both were creating a new result--a new experience that matched their desires. Their attention to changing their own thoughts and beliefs was changing the outward manifestation of them.

To <u>manifest</u> is to transform our thoughts, beliefs, ideas, and even fantasies into objective reality where our senses can experience them. Sometimes we do this consciously. More often we do this unconsciously, and it may take some effort to discover the thought pattern that preceded the manifested experience or object. This is a simple concept to understand but it is not always easy to put into practice. Old habits of belief and perception die hard.

Assuming responsibility for what manifests in one's life can be challenging, particularly if for a lifetime one has been socialized to look outside for the satisfaction of needs and desires. Yet, through an awareness of what our beliefs are and how they operate and manifest in our daily life we can enjoy real freedom. For then we are no longer dependent on some outside power, whether a person or circumstance, to satisfy our needs and create our happiness.

In this book, we will journey down a path of discovery, exploring these concepts and how they operate in everyday life. We'll learn how to create parking places just where we want them, how to manifest the perfect job, and how to attract the mate we've always wanted.

A Manifestation Group

Journeying with us will be a group of twenty people who put aside for a period of one year their belief that much of what happened to them in their daily life was outside their control. For this twelve-month period they "tried on" the belief in self responsibility.

An Invitation

The group members represented a variety of occupational backgrounds--sales persons, secretaries, an artist, dance teacher, computer repairman, retired chemist, nurse, teacher, editor, house cleaner, engineer, and interior designer. Almost all had at least some college education. About half belonged to and attended a church or synagogue. About a third were married, half divorced, or separated and the remainder were never married. The median age was forty-five but the overall range went from twenty-five to sixty-five. Though most participants rated their health "good" or "excellent," only half used these terms to describe their financial situations. Also, three-quarters of the group was female. Perhaps this imbalance supports the stereotype of males as feeling more comfortable with processes involving the senses and external activity rather than with more intuitive states of consciousness.

The group members had many different reasons for wanting to participate in this project. Some were simply attracted to the principle of self-growth. They saw the group as an opportunity to develop a kind of spiritual expansion and awareness. Another person saw this opportunity as an outgrowth of a lifelong process of growth.

I have been on a spiritual search on some level since I was a little girl. In the past few years I have suddenly met people with whom I could

15

> share the feelings and questions I've had inside for so long and who have had valuable information and insights to share. It feels so right. I feel like I was drawn to your project as the next step for my growth and heightened awareness. It's so wonderful to be in such a safe, accepting, mind and soul-expanding group.

Most of the participants were more specific: They wanted to learn about a process that they had always suspected operated in their life or were looking for a way to advance their previously sporadic practice of this process. "I feel I need to put more time and conscious effort into it," said one. "I need the support of a group and the discipline of writing." Another person believed, she said, "that we do manifest our lives negatively or positively via our thoughts, and I thought it would be fun to prove it."

One of the participants had been using this process but hoped "the discipline involved in participating in the project will help me accomplish my goals." The project was an answer to a desire to find support and like-minded people for a process one participant already "knew" was operating in her life.

> I feel I have been ever pulled in this direction from childhood on and now it is all coming home to roost. I have been struck from time to time during my life with my powers of wishing and willing and often shied away from believing in them because of the culture. About eight to ten

years ago, when I began to meditate, my life really changed because of what I manifested. Getting into this project was a manifestation--a wish.

All members entered the group with some belief in the effectiveness of the manifestation process, but within this general framework of belief was a wide range of doubt and qualification. Some had successfully manifested for years. "I have always believed if you want something hard enough and power it up enough you can have it." Another person believed a "person's attitude has everything to do with how she experiences the world. I believe a person creates their own reality." Some mentioned the importance of being able to visualize what you want and having faith. "Your whole being must not have any fear."

Others mentioned examples in their life when they "knew" they had created their experience and now wanted to become more conscious of this process and expand its usefulness. An artist noted that when he had taken the time to write and visualize, "art jobs suddenly popped out of nowhere." He hoped "to force or encourage myself to ask more questions and keep a journal." And still another person said he had "visualized my girlfriend about two months before I met her. She was exactly to a tee what I described."

An amusing incident happened to a woman who kept visualizing some renovations in her home that she could not afford. After about a year of her "off-and-on" visualizations, a water hose broke in her home flooding the areas of the house that needed renovation. Her insurance company covered the costs for the entire repair work, including the changes she wanted. She had never visualized <u>how</u> the renovation would be done or financed. She simply had imagined how the home would appear after the renovations were completed.

Another participant had wanted to work for a small publisher in Vermont. Through several synchronous events of being in the right place at the right time, he did get the job. In another experience he reported how he "also used to blame my boss or my wife for making my life difficult. When they left my life I found I was still creating much unhappiness <u>so I knew I was the creator of those emotions.</u>" This is an interesting illustration of how we learn responsibility for negative as well as positive events that happen to us in our lives.

Many participants expressed doubts about their own abilities as manifestors as well as about the process of manifesting itself. "My intellect understands this," said one, "but the rest of my being is still in the process of accepting this reality." Another person <u>wanted</u> to believe it "because it makes the most sense to me of any model for life I've seen" but needed to demonstrate its effectiveness. Still another participant thought "some things are out of your control. But I would like to be convinced that everything is under our control."

Other members felt one could manifest certain objects or experiences but they were uncertain how far this process could be taken.

It has been easier to manifest new gloves, trips abroad and a new apartment than to create a relationship. That seems much more elusive.

To some degree I believe you make things happen for yourself and I do think there are happenings out of my control. I'm still not sure I can make a lost cassette tape reappear. I need more convincing of that type of manifesting.

A participant who doubted her own abilities and "worthiness" to have what she desired looked to the group to provide the support, encouragement, and guidance necessary to create her life.

On some level I have always known that it was up to me to create what I wanted in my life. I just always felt too afraid and unworthy to try it. However, now I'm at a point in my life where I'm determined to take responsibility for making my life better. I believe this project will provide a good avenue to pursue my goals of self and life improvement.

As we will see in later sections of this book, faith in one's own abilities and a feeling of deservedness are essential conditions for successful manifesting.

Finally, there were group members who had been only vaguely conscious of the manifestation process but wanted to explore this more consciously and objectively. Several participants had been aware of synchronistic patterns from time to time. As one person noted: "I haven't done any conscious manifesting, although there have been times when something I had been thinking about came into being in a way where I seemed to be at the right place at the right time." Noted another subject, "What I believe usually happens, good or bad. Lately, I have been manifesting goals I haven't given a lot of thought to. I might describe something I want, forget about it, and later I would get what I wanted." The process of "forgetting" or detaching from a desire as illustrated by this experience is another condition for manifesting that will be explored in this book.

At the beginning of the project, the group members shared certain qualities. First, there had to be an open mindedness to the possibility of being able to manifest one's desires. Faith and trust in the process was essential. Second, there needed to be a willingness to be flexible, to experiment, and to try new ways of looking at life. Life itself became the laboratory and the group member became both the participant and the observer of his or her own process. Finally, commitment to one's own expansion of consciousness, the sharing of information with others and embracing the discipline of regular record keeping was necessary to the success of the project.

Many people at the outset wanted a structure and a supportive setting for their self-exploration. With our guidance, they agreed to discipline themselves by following certain broad guidelines and procedures of observation and record keeping: Their first responsibility was to become aware of their own personal process. Second, they were to share their experiences and learning in monthly meetings with the authors and the other members of the group. The group members used journals or tapes to record their manifestations, describe their own process, and comment on the successes they were having. The authors transcribed this information and organized it to prepare for the book you are now reading. We, too, were doing our own similar process, so we considered ourselves both students and teachers. During the monthly meetings, participants shared experiences and information that could lead to new perceptions and styles of manifesting. The group coordinators encouraged them to challenge and go beyond their own self-imposed beliefs of what was and was not possible but also to respect their own pace and level of comfort. "Playing" with the manifestation process was a theme and we even did some group experimenting around parking places, experiences that we will discuss in the next chapter. One could put considerable time and energy into the manifestation process or very little. Why not try both styles and see what happens? A person with considerable doubts about his ability to create a "perfect" job or ideal mate could start with small manifestations and later advance to larger forms. With practice, one can replace habits of disbelief and doubt with new beliefs about success and worthiness.

The proof was in the created outcomes and experiences. The only thing we stressed as the coordinators was that the participants faithfully record their processes and what they were observing, feeling, and learning. We all agreed that, at least temporarily, we would assume we were creating all events in our lives.

Our Beliefs Direct Our Experience

Many of the participants were not even aware what their beliefs were or how they were reflected in their everyday lives. Sometimes they had to look at events in their lives and then work "back" to discover the beliefs that created those events. Occasionally they would find that their personal beliefs conflicted. Paul, for example, knew the power of the mind to heal the body because he had read of the experiments reviewed earlier. Yet, on another level, he felt only a doctor and a prescribed medication could cure the illness or disability that was affecting him.

All belief systems create limits. Until 1954, nearly everyone thought running a four-minute mile was impossible. Yet once Roger Bannister broke that barrier, many runners were able to repeat his achievement. We can exchange one belief system for another with fewer limits. By becoming aware of our own beliefs and thoughts and the way they create our experiences, we can increase the self-empowerment and control in our lives.

In a recent publication on overcoming addictions, the Serenity Principle, Joseph Bailey urges us to become conscious that we are not our own thoughts but the creators of our thoughts. Our belief system is not our "self," he writes, but "a filter through which we interpret life." We tend to look for and find whatever has validated our previous view of reality. "When we are unaware that our thoughts create reality," says Bailey, "we become victims of our belief system and can only respond through our habits." It is not our problems or our past experiences in themselves that cause our unhappiness. The cause is how we choose to perceive an event or experience. When we realize that our thoughts, beliefs and perceptions are voluntary we are free to create positive thoughts and thus positive experiences.

Only Experience Will Truly Convince

When Sally thinks back to the first time she really felt she had created a desired objective through thought, she was only just beginning to become aware of the power of the process. The events she describes took several months to unfold but she had no doubt she was the creator of all that happened even if she could not understand the process or validate it scientifically.

> I had just seen the movie <u>Amadeus</u> on television and had made a videotape of it since I was a big fan of Mozart. There was a particular scene in the film taken from the opera "The Abduction from the Seraglio" that I fell in love with. Only a very small portion of a particular aria was presented in the film itself. Night after night I played it back enjoying the brief melody while still hoping that someday I could hear not only this whole aria but the entire opera. There was no obsession but a simple wish or gentle desire. My enthusiasm waned somewhat over time as other events and musical experiences captured my fancy but I would still remember this experience and hope that someday I would get to hear more of the opera.

About six months after first seeing <u>Amadeus,</u> on a Sunday morning, Sally by chance tuned in to a public radio classical music broadcast just at the time they were introducing a new selection. She almost never listened to this station on Sunday morning. Yet this Sunday, for some reason, she turned it on.

> At the moment I tuned in they said they were going to play highlights from the opera "Abduction from the Seraglio" by Mozart. Had I tuned in a few minutes later I might never have known what I was listening to and certainly would not have recorded the music, since I only

knew the one short aria from the movie. Also, I had an errand to do during the presentation itself, and would probably have turned off the radio before running the errand. As it was, I recorded it while I was away. Three months later the entire production was telecast on two public television stations which I receive. Again, I just "happened" to notice in the television part of the paper that it was being shown that day. I do not regularly read what is being shown on television each day. Furthermore, three months later a classmate in a group meeting just happened to tell me that a live production of this particular opera was being performed in Montreal about a two hour drive from my home. I should mention that this opera is not one of the most popular operas and certainly is one of the lesser known productions of Mozart.

To an outsider, all these experiences could be coincidence. However, Sally had no doubt herself that these were not coincidence because she personally experienced these events. The wonder of the unfoldment and the associated feelings of awe and joy were impossible for her to convey in words, she told us. She simply "knew" there was a connection between her desire and the manifested experience. And once she recognized it, she began to see this pattern emerging again and again.

For this reason, we encourage you to experiment with the process yourself. This book will not try to persuade with masses of scientific evidence, as a scientific report might try to do. Yet if you are open to experimentation, are willing to explore your own beliefs, and are committed to becoming the creator rather than the victim of your life, then you will convince <u>yourself</u> of your own power. You will become your own best observer, experimenter, and scientist. As you read about the experiences of the twenty participants in this project, you will learn that there are many ways and many methods that can result in successful manifestations. We invite you to join us on a journey, a journey that can result in a newfound awareness of your own power and creativity to shape your life. You will have an opportunity to share the triumphs and setbacks, the insights and techniques and, most of all, to share the transformations of self and perception that this group of people experienced over the course of a year. Keep in mind, however, that it will not be the stories or incidents in this book that will convince you of the power of thought in creating your reality. Only your willingness to take responsibility for your thoughts and to try some actual exercises for yourself will ultimately prove the value of the process. So enjoy the accounts of others--but use them as suggestions and inspirations for your own manifestation exercises and experiences. Use whatever information seems most helpful to you, while not being limited by what is presented, in your own personal quest for self-empowerment.

Chapter Two

MANIFESTING FOR FUN

So how does one begin the process of manifesting what one wants? First, remember that there are no hard and fast techniques or cardinal rules to follow. You need only be open to the possibility that you can create your desires. As we mentioned earlier, pretending that you have this power can be sufficient to get started. Play with this principle and watch for results. Become the experimenter and observe the outcome of your experiment. You might keep a daily journal of your experiences and observations to encourage a routine of daily experiments and to provide a record of your successes.

Don't try too hard. Manifesting should be fun. Even when things don't "seem" to work out, pay attention to the conditions under which you were manifesting. Were you happy, sad, anxious, desperate? What mood do you seem to be in when you are most successful? Become an observer of yourself. But do it with a sense of curiosity and fun.

When you start off, your goal should be clear. Pick some goal that will give you immediate feedback, where you don't have a lot of emotion invested in a particular outcome. That is, whether you get what you desire or not doesn't affect how you feel about yourself or your life. Also, pick some goal that is unlikely to happen just by chance but is still well within your belief system of possible outcomes. If you select a goal that you believe is absolutely impossible to achieve through your own will power, then it will not manifest because of this belief.

The easiest kinds of experiments to begin with for the members of the manifestation group were part of the normal routine of daily life. Life was the laboratory where we would discover our power in small ways to create our desires. Through such experiences we gained confidence and a belief in ourselves to move on to more challenging goals and dreams.

Most group manifestors began by visualizing. Probably you do this all the time without even being very conscious of it. For example, most of us have an image of what we want when we go shopping. When I shop for food I usually picture the item while making out my grocery list. If the store is familiar to me, I may even picture the item in a certain area. If it is an article of clothing, I may picture the color and style and fabric as well as a likely location where I will find it.

Visualizing Parking Places

Visualization, as practiced by the group members, was only a somewhat more conscious and focused application of this very common human ability to see in the mind the object or experience desired.

One of the first objects the manfestation group chose to experiment with was parking places. Many people need a place to park every day, so a manifestor can gather plenty of evidence in a short time. And few people have a great deal of emotion or ego attached to the outcome. (If they have, as we will see later, it can effect the outcome.)

Manifestors usually chose a desired parking place where their success in the past was infrequent--this gave them a basis for comparison. Getting these parking places was possible, but not probable. It was a good example of something that would be unlikely to occur by chance.

Some manifestors describe their results:

I hadn't ever really worked on a parking place so last Wednesday on my way to your house I thought I'd try it. I always ended up parking on the next block whenever I went to your house in the past. So I pictured a space directly across from your house, and concentrated on this in a very positive way and just simply decided the spot would be there. Well, I pulled down your road and there was that parking spot. It wasn't up or down a little but directly across from your front door! Ah the power of positive thinking.

Every time I go to Burlington I have a tough time finding a parking place. I like to park at City Market. I decided there would be a parking place right in front of City Market.

There never ever is. I didn't work on it too hard. I decided it would be there. I turned the corner and there it was right in front of City Market. I love it!

I wanted to manifest the best possible place near a place I knew would be busy on a Friday night. The chances of getting a place were near nil at that time. I projected a place right in front or very near by. As I was driving down College street someone backed out right across the street. The guy was pulling out just as I was getting to my destination. You talk about energy. That was incredible!

I was manifesting I would find the perfect place at the entrance to the shopping mall. I was at the mall to participate in a Christmas concert and needed to be close. The closest car to the entrance mall pulled out just when I needed it. I said, "Yes, yes!" Other drivers wanted it, but I was there first. I couldn't believe it.

I needed to get to my haircut appointment at 9 A.M. where it is almost impossible to find a place at that hour. I was running ten minutes late and needed a place. I "put it out" and knew it would be there. I "saw" the spot right out in front of the building in my mind. It was a brief visualization. I didn't have time to run around finding a place. I got the only place on that block, right where I had visualized it.

Two days after Thanksgiving, I had to go to Ames department store and I decided what spot I wanted. I pictured I wanted to park at the fourth spot down from the handicapped spot to the right of Ames. Sure enough I got to Ames at 11:30 in the morning and got that exact spot.

Several themes characterize these parking place successes. First, the manifestors' intents were very clear. They wanted specific areas that were convenient to their destinations. Some wanted very specific locations and, in the last case, only one location would do.

Second, all knew from past experience that getting these places was not likely, but neither was it impossible. All were positive they would get them. Doubt was not present for these manifestors. (Later, we will examine situations where doubt was present, and what the consequences were.)

Third, little effort was involved in the visualizations. One "didn't work on it too hard." For another, "it was only a brief visualization." They had confidence they would be successful. They just "knew" or "decided" the spots would be there.

Finally, almost all of the successful manifestors appreciated their own success. Even though they were confident, they still "couldn't believe it," found it "incredible," and "loved it." Doubts came back only after the experiment was concluded. The manifestors had "parked" their doubts off to the side during the experiment.

In a variation on parking places, two people who were overparked visualized having no parking tickets on their windshields.

> I forgot to put money in a meter I know is patrolled frequently. I tried to visualize "no ticket" on the windshield. There was no ticket. The parking meter froze so the arm couldn't come up. I spent a couple of additional hours downtown without a ticket. I had a freebie.

> I visualized a parking spot on Cherry Street and found it. I was gone much longer than the meter allowed. I visualized a windshield with no ticket. Not only was there no ticket, but there was time left on the meter. I parked there for almost two hours and the meter only registered about 45 minutes. A few weeks later, I manifested the same place and again I stayed longer than the money I put in justified. And although the meter had expired when I returned, I didn't have a ticket, which was what I had visualized.

Fun with Everyday Experiences

Opportunities exist every day to create more joy and less effort while going about the business of daily living. Manifesting also makes life more interesting. Each situation can become an experiment in personal power, as we see in the examples that follow. The first involves a manifestor who enjoyed using his mind to move traffic out of his way while driving. He used a tape recorder in his car and described the incidents as they happened. His enthusiasm and excitement was evident on the tape. The other incidents require little additional comment.

> There are are ten cars in front of me following a large truck. I am going to expand my energy space out and have the way open up. [pause] There goes the truck! It just pulled off. I also have been losing cars and there are only three or four cars in front of me now. One car turned into a driveway and another turned off and there is now no one in front of me. It is amazing! Just amazing!--[10 minutes later] A dump truck just pulled out in front of me. Bingo! Three miles down the road the truck turned off. It worked again. I'm all clear. [5 minutes later]---Now there is a bucket loader in front of me. Here goes number three. This one took only thirty seconds.

> I needed to call my husband at the Naval Reserve Center. In the past I have always gotten either a busy signal or no answer and it has really frustrated me. Today I kept getting busy signals, so I began visualizing the person who answers the phone hanging up from a call and answering mine. It worked! Of all the times I've tried to reach my husband in the past, I'd only gotten through once before.

> United Parcel Service can be a zoo right before Christmas; as a matter of fact it always has been whenever I've been there at this time of the year. As I was driving there I began thinking how wonderful it would be if there

was no line when I got to UPS. I actually visualized two people ahead of me, which at this time of year is absurd. Well, much to my delight, when I walked into UPS at 11:00 in the morning there were two people ahead of me. They were both being waited on, so I was the next person in line. Hurrah! I couldn't believe it but it was delightful and I was very grateful.

Lately I have this annoying problem--I have to run out of the movie I am watching to go to the bathroom, especially if I've been out and had a drink first. A couple of weeks ago I had dinner at a Chinese restaurant including a beer and some tea. Just as the movie started I told my body that all the cells would retain their water and my bladder would remain empty. I felt confident that my body could do this. Well, I didn't even have to go to the bathroom after the movie. My friend and I went to a bar for a drink. I still didn't have to go. I got home at 1:30 A.M. and I still didn't have to go! I tried this last week and it worked again! This will become an opening-credit movie ritual for me from now on.

A footnote to the incident with UPS: This experimenter also tried visualization at UPS on a second occasion. This time she visualized only one person ahead of her. (Perhaps her previous experience gave her confidence to push her belief system a bit further.) She did find just one person ahead of her, but that one person had dozens of packages to mail. She reports, "A few moments went by. Then a second cashier appeared and I was rushed through rather quickly." She got what she had asked for, but what she really wanted was to get through quickly. She was fortunate that some part of her knew this was her real desire. Perhaps a lesson here is to be careful what you ask for--you are likely to get it.

As she was leaving UPS, she noticed "six to eight people behind me waiting to send their parcels." Also, the reason she had to make a second trip to UPS so soon after the first was suddenly clear. "The gift had come later than I had expected, forcing me to go back so that I could experience . . . success in getting through as I wanted to."

The reader can probably sense the enjoyment this woman was having with manifesting. She was playing with her power. Making a second trip, which might have been an aggravation, instead became an opportunity to repeat her previous experiment. She was challenging but not overextending her belief about what might be possible, creating only one person in line the second time instead of two. She had no overwhelming need to create a short line. Rather her attitude was, "Wouldn't it be wonderful if?"

Manifesting Objects and Articles

How often have you desired some object and not known where to find it? Then, when you are not looking for it, it presents itself, often in an unexpected place. Whether the item is small or large, the process is the same.

I wanted a straw hat. I visualized it but did not give it a great deal of effort or put in a lot of detail. I knew I would run into it, perhaps at a garage sale. As I was backing out of the Grand Union parking lot, I noticed a straw hat sitting in the middle of the road. I looked around but nobody was claiming it. So now I have a new straw hat and it didn't cost me anything.

I wanted a watch pin to wear on my blouse. I can't wear a regular watch because it irritates my skin. I had never seen one for sale for less than $25. I had put it in my 'want file' in the back of my head. I thought about it three or four times a week. It was not so much visual. I did not restrict it to how it would look. Yesterday while running into a department store to use the ladies' room, I saw it for $9.95. I had a variety to choose from.

I was invited to a formal dance. I knew exactly the dress I wanted to wear. I wanted it to be tight fitting in the upper part of the body and then come out and it should cost less than $100. I pictured this dress but did not think about it too much. I just decided I was going to get it. I had made up my mind. I went into a store and the first dress I looked at was the dress. There were two of them--one short sleeve and one long sleeve. That was the only decision I had to make. The clerk said, "Get the long sleeve one." And it was only $60. I loved it and got tons of compliments. It looked great!

I had been visualizing day after day the early arrival of the costumes so it would come in time for the important group picture. They had told me they would come by May 14 but I said they had to come by May 2. I put a sign on the front door of the studio on May 2 telling him to leave the costumes at the studio. The chances of him coming on that afternoon were slim but I visualized it again and again and again. And that is how it happened.

I wanted a red car with a sunroof, sporty, with a stereo system, that would appeal to my inner child. When I finally found the car, the salesman was sorry but it had been promised to someone else. That was Friday. Over the weekend I never doubted that somehow this car was going to be mine. I envisioned it parked in the driveway to my house. I saw myself driving it to Virginia, where my parents live. Monday morning I received a call from the car dealership. I was told that it was a miracle that the deal had worked out for me. Not only had the car been promised to another individual, but unknown to the dealer the car had also been offered to a wholesale buyer who had the second option on the car. This buyer had been reluctant to make an offer, and by the time he came to buy the car it was already mine.

A straw hat blowing on the street. The perfect dress found in the first store. A delivery of costumes on an afternoon when there was no likelihood of delivery. A car promised to two other people suddenly available.

These individuals had no doubt they created their "luck." (Actually, no one in the group ever uses the word luck.) The individual who wanted the red car somehow "knew it was going to be mine." And the person who expected the costume delivery was so sure it was coming on the day she had determined it would come that she left a sign for the UPS delivery man to deliver it to her studio. There was some variation in effort--from the woman who wanted the dress and "did not think about it too much" to the person who visualized the UPS delivery "day after day after day."

Finally we present a manifestation that involved more than one person. Does it hasten a manifestation if someone is helping you? In this case two sisters were involved in manifesting a pedestal sink. The sister who had wanted it for the previous two years affirmed in her mind "a white pedestal sink in good condition at a reasonable price. Every time I went into the bathroom I visualized the sink there." Her sister was also manifesting for her at a price between $100 and $250. "I picture myself using it and how it will look in her bathroom."

About three weeks after both sisters first began manifesting in earnest, the sister who wanted the sink was on a drive with her husband. "My husband said, 'Think pedestal sink,' as we drove up a long hill. As we came down the other side, there it was, outside in a yard. It was in good condition and cost $175. This is really neat."

For two years before they joined forces and used the technique of visualization, she was unable to locate the sink. Doing a daily visualization, they located it within three weeks. It is also interesting that the husband intuited its location, cuing them in so they would not speed past it. Note also that the price they paid was exactly halfway between the minimum and maximum amounts they had agreed to pay for the sink.

Visualization for Athletes

In Chapter 1 we mentioned studies that document the effectiveness of visualization for enhancing athletes' abilities in sports. It can be almost as effective as spending the same amount of time in physical training. The body simply does not seem able to distinguish between the activity experienced and the activity vividly imagined.

Every so often I would bring the lacrosse team together and have the girls take a few deep breaths. I would then lead them through a guided visualization of a play or move we were having problems with. I noticed every time we did that they were so tuned in and things clicked. They really could do things with ease and grace. It was incredible. This became a ritual. Before games I would lead them through a visualization of a game-related situation where we would see the ball in front of them. They would pick it up perfectly, cradle it perfectly, pass it perfectly and eventually score. I would ask them to feel the joy of running down the field and scoring.

After we did that together I would have them do it on their own quietly.

My daughter was having problems riding the horse correctly. Every night just before bed she and I both visualized riding the horse the way the instructor had told her to. This meant putting her foot in the stirrups, riding the horse holding legs and arms properly, getting into a run with the horse and seeing herself as the perfect horseback rider and floating with it. I reminded her to do it first thing when she got up in the morning and the last thing when she went to bed at night. We did it together for a week. Her next riding lesson was phenomenal. Her teacher couldn't believe how connected she was with the riding--such as how she held her hands. Remember, she hadn't ridden at all in a week. She had only practiced it in her mind. She was right on cue. She had done exactly as the teacher had told her. Prior to this visualization exercise she had had a persistent problem.

One nice thing about this exercise is that you can, as with parking places, obtain direct feedback in a short time. You have a clear memory of what the problem is and recognize that practice isn't helping that much. You do the visualization exercise and watch for the results. In the horse-riding episode, the daughter did not even have an opportunity for physical practice. Yet her teacher confirmed her progress.

Money and Business

How often have you thought about winning the lottery or have you just "known" there would be enough money to pay the bills at the end of the month? Perhaps you wonder how you can increase your sales with some simple visualizations. The following cases illustrate these examples.

I always wanted to go to California. When I would get magazines I'd clip a couple of California pictures and 'dream weave' a story about it with me in it. I would also focus on a picture of a particular room I wanted to stay in. I used the room visualization as a concrete focus or symbol for the trip to California. At a wine and food festival there was a grand prize of a trip to California and private tours of vineyards. I bought four tickets and began powering up my mental movie. About half an hour before the drawing, a little voice said to buy six more tickets. It would not relent. Six tickets cost $24. I only had $25 in my wallet. I bought those tickets and won the trip.

I've been having trouble paying my bills this past month. The only time I really make any fast cash is when I am waitressing. The past few nights I have been envisioning myself making a certain amount of money each night. Each time that I have done this I have made the predicted amount and was able to pay my bills. That is why I don't get stressed when I think I won't have enough cash by the end of the month.

I sell advertising space. Before I approach a potential client, I imagine them happy to see me and excited about my product, and I imagine them saying 'Yes.' It has been going so well for me. I try to approach the interaction with the attitude that I am going to meet some new people and learn about myself through this interaction. In one case I learned that we both had lived in the same city. They asked me about a new computer and I was able to give them advice about one they were trying to fix. I get this feeling we are all people and we all shit in the pot. We are just human beings. I am eliminating fear.

The individual who won the raffle ticket to California, by the way, also got the same rooms she had visualized. "Both rooms were exactly as pictured," she said, even though she and her husband arrived in California on Memorial Day Weekend without reservations.

Notice that the person who used visualization to make a sale defused the "need" to make a sale by focusing on the human qualities of the potential clients. She saw them as "interesting" people who would help her learn about herself.

There was a history of negativity with some of her former clients, and she assumed at first the new owners would express the same hostility towards her. She caught herself doing this, however, and projected instead a positive, friendly first meeting. It did turn out to be the way she envisioned it. Perhaps it would have happened without the visualization, but at the very least she gained the courage to meet the new owners instead of simply giving up.

Conclusion

By now we hope you are inspired by the examples from this chapter and want to try some manifesting of your own. True appreciation of your power, as we have said, can only come from your own experiments. Be sure to choose goals that do not go against your belief about what is possible. Pick something just beyond what you think might occur by reasonable chance. Watch your desires and see what happens. Also, look at each present experience or object in your life. Might it have originated in a previous thought of yours? Above all, have fun in whatever you choose to manifest.

CHAPTER 3

SOME BASIC MANIFESTING PRINCIPLES

How Much Detail Should You Give Your Goals?

You have now had some experience manifesting parking places and articles of clothing and are ready to create something a bit more complex. Most of the examples we have used so far have been relatively small and concrete. In fact, when they were starting out, most people in the project chose goals that were direct and uncomplicated.

> This morning I started thinking about getting a hat. At 8:15 A.M., I decided I was going to find a hat today--one that fits, stays on and looks nice. At 12:40 P.M. I found it and I've never seen a hat like it before. I have about three plain straw hats, but this hat is made out of a heavier material and it was reduced from $14 to $6.

> I wanted an affectionate toy poodle because they are not allergen causing and don't shed. I couldn't afford one from the pet shop, so I put out to the universe that if anyone in this area has a toy poodle they wanted to get rid of for any reason, I wanted to know about it. In less than a week I saw an ad in a weekly newspaper saying toy

poodle for sale. They had to get rid of her because their daughter beat up on the dog.

These are fairly small items and do not seem to require a great deal of thought or effort. However, for some items or experiences, you may want to be much more specific and detailed. Larger goals almost seem to invite elaboration. Taking a vacation can often require some careful planning. Choosing an apartment is a big investment, both in terms of money and lifestyle.

My ski vacation in Austria had to have great snow and sun. I want the right flight and to have enough money for everything. There must be good weather for traveling and convenient luggage transfers. Also I want fun people to ski with and go out with. I want to have a great time!

I would try to jog every day, and while jogging I said, I want a light, quiet, warm apartment. I also made a list of essentials and a list of preferences and pictured myself sitting high above the lake with western light on my plants and a kitchen behind me, the bedroom in the back. When I picture my future apartment in my mind it feels real good!

By their own assessment, both of these individuals were quite successful. The apartment manifestor reports, "I got all my essentials and most of the preferences. The things I got that I hadn't listed were strange--like no square rooms and a four-foot-high closet."

This last point raises an interesting question about manifesting details. What happens to those aspects of the object or experience that you do not specify? Do you have "to cover all the bases," so to speak, or risk receiving some features you really don't want? Here are two examples that illustrate some of the potential problems of becoming more precise and detailed in your manifestations.

I wanted my credit card to be clear. I got in the mail an offer to switch credit cards; they would pay off the old card to switch to their card at a lower interest rate. I switched and got exactly what I asked for--"a clear credit card." Of course, I realize now what I should have asked for and really wanted was a paid- off card with no debt.

It seems that whatever was lacking in one relationship would appear in the next. For example, if I was with someone who was not masculine enough, I would focus on that, and my next encounter with someone would be with a very masculine man. But there would be other things wrong because I had only focused on that one quality.

At a workshop on June 24, 1988, we had to write down a goal we wanted to reach by the following year and how we would go about it. My main goal was to have a stable, fulfilling relationship by June 26, 1989. I was not desperate. Basically I had no expectations and just enjoyed the moment. Periodically I would think about what I thought might be an ideal relationship and came to the conclusion that a relationship similar to the one I had with my best friend. On July 5, 1988 he walked into the store. I realize I manifested this relationship, which is very much like my relationship with my best friend. What I never thought to ask for was someone who is sensuous and health conscious. This experience has taught me to be more general about what I ask for and to trust that the universe will take care of my specific needs and desires.

I had thought that teaching cartooning would be fun and profitable as a job. It took over a year for my application to be looked at. In that time period I forgot about the position and focused on my progress as a caricaturist. When the opportunity arrived, I suddenly thought of excuses for not doing it: I had no car, it would interfere with other jobs, and my political mouth. This is a case of attracting something you don't quite want or it isn't really the best thing. Usually it takes a while to realize it isn't what you really want.

In previous examples the subjects were fairly clear on what they wanted and were happy with the results. Aspects of the apartment on which the manifestor did not focus were "strange" but did not mar her overall satisfaction. But the group members did not always know what they wanted. In the above examples, both manifestors got just what they "thought" they wanted, but ultimately they were not so happy with the results. This brings up the issue of clarity of goal--be careful what you select to manifest because you <u>will</u> get it.

The first case is just an amusing small example. The manifestor got exactly what she asked for, which was to clear her credit card of debt. What she really wanted, however, was no debt. In the second case, of the romantic partner, the subject had not clearly established in her own mind the kind of person she wanted to attract. But her experience does provide her with information that she can use to create a new manifestation. She is like a scientist who tries out several formulas until she hits upon the answer. We can read about or tell others about the kind of relationship or job we desire. But at some point we may need to "try on" or experience a particular kind of relationship or job to find out if this is truly what we want.

This manifestor also realized she liked "exotic" men: "I do need to focus on a type of man I could really have a relationship with, and not just exciting encounters." For much of her early adult life, she liked adventurous brief flings. But when she wanted to create a more stable, lasting relationship, her early desires kept interfering with her new creation. She also had much attachment and anxiety around this manifestation: "Those small affairs or encounters seemed easy to manifest because there wasn't a lot of emotion around the preceding thoughts. There is a lot of emotion around trying to find my soul mate."

The third person thought she wanted a relationship much like the one she had with her best friend, and she did create it. It had many admirable qualities, but she left out the strong romantic component, which was not part of her relationship with her best friend. One reaction would have been to try to be so specific that she covered all the bases, so to speak. Her alternative reaction was to trust some higher power or what she called "the universe" to take into account all her desires and needs and come up with a suitable partner.

Finally, the kind of job the artist wanted at one time did not appeal to him a year later. We are always evolving, and there is often a gap between our initial desires and projections and the eventual consequences. Even though the artist turned the job down, he probably learned something about himself by going through the process.

As a footnote to the story about the toy poodle, the manifestor later found out that the dog was very destructive when left alone. She damaged the curtains and literally trashed the apartment one evening, necessitating that she be returned to the former owner. The manifestor had not asked for a dog who was willing to be left alone in the apartment.

After one of the group members became divorced, he drew up a list of characteristics that he thought he would find desirable in a new partner. He began to fantasize what it would be like to meet such a woman. Within a couple of months, he met a very attractive and compatible colleague. She shared his interests, loved sports and music, and enjoyed playing tennis on a regular basis.

Had I been recording my manifestations at that time, I would have seen that she almost perfectly matched my checklist. However, one characteristic I had left off my list was sexual orientation. Much to my frustration, she was a lesbian.

How, then, do we deal with the issue of getting more than we bargained for in our manifestations? After all, it is almost impossible to cover all contingencies ahead of time.

Some manifestors dealt with this issue by omitting many specifics about the desired object or experience and instead focusing on a central feeling of what it would be like to have the object or experience. What would you be experiencing if you had just obtained your desire? A similar approach is simply to <u>trust</u> that some higher power or authority, either within or outside yourself, knows what is best for you.

I am trying to live more out of trusting my process and the universe than consciously trying to shape the future, which is new for me. I think I have tried too hard in the past to hold onto conscious control of things. I now feel the best course for me is to manifest in generalities because I want to be open to possibilities that may be much greater than what I come up with on my own but which wouldn't have occurred to me.

Nowadays, whenever I describe some specific interests I wish to share with my ideal partner, I always make sure to include some general characteristics such as shared joy, laughter and all forms of intimacy and companionship. I still include the most important specific characteristics but I also try to imagine what it would <u>feel</u> like to be in an ideal relationship. I try to remain open to possibilities which I might consciously overlook that could give me much enjoyment and stimulation.

Another consideration, when you decide to manifest a detailed "laundry list," is whether those desired elements come from your intrinsic needs or from outside expectations. For example, one manifestor wanted a job that would not interfere with the time her husband worked or the time when her children would be home from school. She also wanted a good salary so she could supplement her husband's income. She found a job that fit these criteria exactly, yet she eventually turned it down because it involved fund raising which she knew would be stressful to her. She then found a job working within a school system that also had these characteristics, but she quit after one year. Eventually, she realized that the job she manifested had to be interesting and challenging to <u>her</u>, and she began to focus less exclusively on what she thought her family needed.

So often we look outside, to the needs of others or to the values expressed within our culture, for guidance in choosing appropriate goals. When we ignore our internal interests and desires, we feel dissatisfied and confused.

Towards the end of this book we will discuss the value of what we learn from the manifestation process even when the desired manifestation does not seem to "work out" the way we expected. Attaining goals is really only a small part of the pleasure we can experience along the path of goal manifesting because attaining today's goal only leads to new goals tomorrow. As we appreciate the process of manifesting and what we learn from it, we add a great deal of adventure and enjoyment to life.

Although he felt at first frustrated, the manifestor who ended up with a friendship instead of a romantic relationship with a gay woman learned how to be intimate in nonromantic ways, which helped him relate to other women. Over time he developed many wonderful close friendships with women, which helped alleviate some of the loneliness and provide some of the companionship he originally believed could come only from a romantic relationship. There are many forms in which our desires can be addressed if we do not limit ourselves.

Techniques of Manifesting
Visualization

In Chapter 2, we explored a wide range of manifested experiences. Almost all of them used some form of visualization--the most popular technique used by the group members. Manifestors created a picture in their minds of their desired outcomes. They visualized, for example, "being open and loving while teaching," "a sporty red car in my driveway," "happy clients," "how to cradle and pass at the same time," and "cells retaining water so my bladder would remain empty."

Each person achieved the visualized outcome, in most cases with a minimal amount of effort. One manifestor reported, "For smaller, less potent visualizations, sometimes all it takes is a well-thought out flicker in the mind." Another said that for a minor goal, "I just see it happening in my mind's eye and then keep my real eyes open to recognize the results. If I want to talk to someone, I 'see' them calling me on the phone. Usually they do."

One manifestor was very fearful of facing her boss and telling her she was resigning her job. She realized, she said, "that by expecting negativity that is what I would create."

I pictured pink light, which is the color of love, all through my boss and the situation and the office. I pictured giving up my fears and giving her a hug. It was fantastic. She talked to me for over an hour about how she understood where I was now in my life and admitted she didn't want me to leave.

The salesperson also employed this technique before approaching a client. She would visualize them "happy to see me and excited about my project and saying 'yes' to my sale."

Another person used a "powered-up" visualization to get rid of some unwanted guests. She called this her "broom technique."

> Three people wanted to stay the night in my house. They were from another part of the state and had other business in the area the next morning. But the timing was not good for me. So I visualized sweeping these people out. It turned out that the engagement they had the next day was canceled.

This is an interesting case because it required the cooperation of a third party, the person with whom they had the appointment and who was the main reason for their staying on at her house.

Verbal Cues

Other manifestators put equal or greater emphasis on verbal cues. One spoke into a tape recorder, saying, for example, "An empty parking space is there for me when I arrive." Another person "thought" about her manifestation and wrote her thoughts in her journal. "Generally, if I don't have time to visualize, I at least remember my major manifestations at least once a day and review them in thought."

Affirmations are verbal statements, oral or written, that express a person's desire.

I didn't know how to start but I knew I had to do something. So I just started talking to myself-- sometimes out loud and sometimes just in my head. I would focus on what I wanted and allow my intuition to formulate what to say. I would say things like, "I am excited and full of energy. I have the perfect job. I love my work." Sometimes I would say things that didn't seem to relate to what I wanted but I would say them anyway. Things like, "I will learn from my experiences. I love people and people love me. I am healthy."

Some used words in a prayerlike fashion. "While driving to work, I would say, 'Day by day I am getting better.'" Another noted, "If I identify a specific goal, I say it out loud to someone and imagine how I will feel when I've achieved it." Many group members used both visual and verbal techniques.

One manifestor needed a change and wanted to retire early. He created a "password" that represented his desire to leave his job.

I didn't think my company would have another early retirement incentive because they had recently had one. It just wasn't in the cards. I began to put together a package of how it would go. I knew that I needed to give this a lot of energy, since this was a big stretch to my beliefs. I used visualization and feeling. I visualized the specifics and felt the essence of the rest. I visualized the amount of pension I needed to receive and that I would retire in one year. The rest of my manifestation focused on what it felt like to be retired. I would feel myself as rested, joyous, full of energy, physically fit, enthusiastic, and loving life.

Once I had this clear intention, I set up a symbol to remind myself to give energy to this manifestation. The symbol was a password that I used several times a day when I signed on to my computer. Every morning when I went to work I would use this password and again another half dozen times during the day. And when I did this, I would savor the moment. I would feel retirement, get a tingly sensation all over my body and gave thanks as if it has already occurred. It took only a second or two. This not only gave energy to my goal, but gave me a much more positive attitude during my day.

I did retire exactly one year later. I received more money than expected. I feel great and give thanks every day.

Seeing the Goal Completed

It is useful to mention that many manifestors visualized their desires or goals in a completed state. One person used visualization to sell her house "by seeing myself at the house closing." Another created a "thought form of how it feels to have the goal already created. I put myself there, in it; I feel it and be it. I visualize it."

A major component is visualizing what I want, since I am a very visual person. With the family room addition I see it as part of the house. With my weight I see myself as the ideal weight. But I also use written affirmations. I talk to myself silently and sometimes aloud about what I want.

First I meditate and then I visualize having what goal I want already realized. Then the recording in a journal seems to give the needed energy a focus.

I begin by writing out my goals, usually in detail, adding material over a period of time. Out of this script I create a meditative visualization in which I experience having achieved my goals.

I write my goals down and re-read them. Before I sleep or just when waking up I mentally review my goals. I visualize moving through the situation from beginning to end and ending with the desired goal.

One of the manifestors has a fairly detailed process that also gives a nice review of what we have considered to this point. First, she states, it is important to "become clear and definite in your desired goal." Second, she "writes it down, allowing room for even greater possibility." She is aware that becoming too focused or specific can limit outcomes and perhaps also result in undesired outcomes, as discussed earlier. Third, she meditates on her goals daily. During this meditation she "sees in detail, color, form and feels with great emotion." During the day she also "affirms verbally whenever the opportunity occurs." This could be a brief verbal or visual recall. Finally, she says, "give heartfelt thanksgiving." Giving thanks for manifested desires is an act of self-love and builds confidence for the time when you desire other goals.

Detaching from Goals: "A Watched Pot Never Boils"

One group member and his sons had been looking forward to a big hockey game. Tickets were on sale at the hockey arena, which was in the same building where he was scheduled to play tennis that afternoon. He would pick up three tickets for that evening's game on the way to playing tennis.

To my amazement and disappointment they sold out by the time I arrived at the ticket counter. How could I go home and tell my sons of this tragedy? Needless to say, I played terrible tennis and hurt my knee to boot lunging for a ball. Near the end of our match I gave up and accepted the inevitable. I had done the best I could. Perhaps I was meant to do something else with my sons that evening, like go to a movie.

On the way out of the arena, I stopped to see one of my former students, who was now the assistant hockey coach, to get some information, since he had asked me to write a recommendation for him to go to graduate school. In our conversation I mentioned my inability to obtain any tickets. He was sorry he hadn't known earlier, he said, because he had given his allotment of free tickets away to friends and relatives.

While we were talking, he received a phone call from one of his friends saying he and his two companions could not make the game that night and he could give the tickets to someone else. With that, he reached inside his desk and pulled out an envelope with three free tickets for that night's game.

Here we see an almost magical timing of events. First, the assistant coach happened to be in his office when the manifestor was leaving the gym. Second, the coach just happened to receive that phone call during the ten minutes the manifestor happened to be in the office. And, finally, the number of tickets he needed was three--the exact number returned to the coach.

The key to this manifestation occurred during the tennis match, when the man gave up and "let go" of his need for the tickets. This willingness to let go and trust is one of the most challenging and yet most important conditions necessary to successful manifesting. There is a tendency to hold on and measure its progress. One manifestor remembers, one cold spring, planting several rows of peas and then digging up a few each day to see if they had sprouted. Of course, each time he dug up a few to check for progress, they died. Just as the gardener must trust that the seeds will grow, so we must detach from the manifesting process and let it happen.

This morning while sitting in my car waiting for the landlord to arrive to show me the apartments, I thought to myself, I hope one of these is it, but if it is not meant to be I can accept that. I was trying not to obsess or involve a lot of ego, which is tough when you desperately need to move out of where you are living and you are looking for a place just for yourself.

I really wanted to be alone. I believe I didn't manifest this wish because I wanted it so much. I was really concerned about the outcome and was so obsessed I didn't manifest what I wanted.

The prizes are always super. I bought twelve tickets and worked and worked on visualizing winning first prize. I pushed and pushed and refused to just turn it over to the universe. I did not win. As I reviewed it tonight, I think I pushed too hard and wanted it much too badly and tried to control, control, control. It doesn't work for me this way. It seems the only way it works is to let go of it.

I wanted him to call me so badly. I want this relationship and I want it now! I'm not being very patient with all this. I have gotten to the point where I am letting another person determine my own happiness instead of determining my own. I keep saying to myself, "He's not calling. What's wrong with me?" It is a control thing with me. I need to be happy with me and know that the right man will come along at the right time. What is interesting is that when I do "let go," he calls. When I feel needy he psychologically picks this up and backs off.

These examples illustrate the challenge of detaching and letting go of the manifestation. For most people, detachment is not an issue around parking places or small objects. The challenge comes when the object is highly desired or needed. Remember the manfestor whose heart was set on those hockey tickets? He was attached because he had waited so long to pick up the tickets. He assumed that his sons would be disappointed, and he would have let them down. So his self-worth was at stake. The woman who wanted her boy friend to call was very needy and feeling unloved. Her neediness drove him away from her, which was the opposite of what she wanted.

It is not easy to say you don't really care if you get the apartment or not when you are desperate to move and the apartment seems perfect for your needs. To trust that your main desire will be realized while the location and timing is out of your hands can be trying. As one of the manifcstors said, "I tried to control, control, control."

Just as I got on the thruway a state policeman pulled alongside going about 55 miles per hour. I and everyone else didn't want to pass. I was feeling increasingly anxious because if I didn't speed up I would be late to my meeting. First, I tried to make him go faster. It was a forcing rather than a flowing. Then I said, "Screw it." I set a certain time to be there. I just knew I would be on time and I relaxed. At that instant of relaxation the police car sped up to 70. It was instantaneous. I let

61

it be okay to let whatever happen happen. It was incredible!

I put out to the universe I needed $100 for a trip to Hampton Beach within three days. I put it out and let it go. The whole process took only a few seconds. The next day my parents came by and gave me my birthday present early. It was $100. I had said to the universe I didn't care where it came from. I could almost feel it coming back to me. I didn't think about it. In previous years, I always got clothes plus maybe 25 or 50 dollars. But I had never gotten $100.

In these two situations, detaching brought the desired result. For the driver, forcing the situation was unsuccessful. He then just focused on the goal of being there at a certain time and trusted that it would occur somehow. It was not a logical decision. For the birthday person, no thinking was involved; in fact, effort could have impeded this manifestation. And she left the form in which the $100 would come entirely open, allowing many options instead of restricting the way in which it manifested.

The next two examples are particularly important because they relate to two goals from which we find it very challenging to detach in our culture. The first is a game, an occasion with only one desired outcome in our competitive society--winning. We all grow up wanting to be champions at whatever we do. Few of us are content simply to do the best we can and enjoy the process of the game itself. Yet the process of detachment can have relevance here.

> I was playing a former champion of the game of cribbage. I kept getting all the good cards. I won all three games. What I noticed is that she was hooked into winning. If you are hooked into having something, it puts negative energy into it and keeps you from having it which is the irony in it. Another time I was playing backgammon, didn't care about the outcome and won the first two games. Then I really wanted to win the last game. My ego got involved. I could feel the loss coming. I tightened up. When you have to get it you tighten up and it gets you. I've seen it many times working in manifesting.

In the next example, we look at romance, an area that often brings up all our insecurities and doubts about ourselves. In some cultures where marriages are arranged and romantic love exists outside of marriage, if it exists at all, there is little ego involvement. But in western society where our marketability as potential mates is paramount, our egos and self-esteem can become quickly involved in any dating relationship. Why aren't we in a relationship? What is wrong with us? Does this indicate we are not desirable?

> Back in 1975 I came to the realization that relationships weren't working for me, even with some trial marriages. I remember trying and trying and being frustrated it wasn't happening. Some

time later at work with a friend of mine, I realized I was forcing it. I was putting too much energy into it. I let the universe take care of it. I gave it up and let go of the forcing of it and said to myself, "Instead of making it happen I will let it happen." About a week later I met [the woman who became] my wife. Right away I was attracted to her. I allowed it to happen. It was not forced and a space was opened for it to occur.

Compare this last account with the woman who wanted her boyfriend to call her and the frustration she created in herself.

The importance of detachment should not be underestimated--yet it can be an elusive concept. It does not mean that you don't have any desires or goals. It means you aren't attached to the process itself. You trust that the manifestation will come when it is appropriate and in whatever form is appropriate. This is not the same as just hoping it will come. It is even all right with you if it doesn't happen at all; perhaps something even better may come in its place. On some occasions what you desire may not be appropriate, a situation that we will discuss in a later section.

This is why we recommend you begin your manifestation experiments with some experiences or desired objects where you don't have a great deal of emotional investment in the outcome. Later, when you manifest items of greater significance you will feel more confident about the process and be less likely to experience problems of attachment.

Knowing, Intuition, and Reason

"I hadn't tried to program for a spot before I left but I <u>knew</u> I was going to find one."

"As soon as I got the phone call I <u>knew</u> I had the job. At the interview she said there were still other people to interview and she would let me know but I knew I had it!"

Over and over again manifestors have used the word <u>knew</u> to explain a part of their process. How did they know something was going to happen? In Chapter 2, how did the dance teacher "know" to put a sign on the front door so that the UPS man could find her when she had no reason to suppose the costumes she had ordered would come on that particular afternoon?

I had a foot I could not walk on. After talking with you I decided to send some energy into my foot to see if I could heal it. At the time I went to bed I couldn't step on it without being in pain. The next morning when I got up I didn't even notice it, and I realized it didn't hurt anymore. I <u>thoroughly believed</u> when I went to bed and woke up it wouldn't hurt any more.

We had only 40 minutes to travel a distance that usually takes a little over one hour to cover. I couldn't pass on the thruway and traveled at less than the normal pace. After leaving the thruway everything went wrong. A car pulled out in front of us going 20 miles per hour. At that time I had a different feeling--like serenity or giving up. I had it real clear in my head that we would be there at ten minutes to eight o'clock, the desired arrival time. Cars will come and go. I don't know how or what the details are, but that is what will happen. I can just sit back. A logging truck pulls out in front of me but I am not anxious. I didn't panic or try to pass because I just knew we would be there at ten of eight. The intersections took longer than normal. I pulled into the parking lot and it was ten of eight, just as we knew it would be. It was an incredible experience! I have driven this many times, and know how long that takes. On the one hand, we were surprised. On the other hand, we weren't. It wasn't logic. It was just knowing.

Physicists would perhaps be able to explain this experience with space-time. But logically, as the above manifestor remarks, there was no way he could explain how they covered that distance in such a short time. Even had they speeded and had no delays from other cars or at intersections it would have been impossible. And to arrive not only in time for work but at the exact minute predicted is remarkable.

Yet many people have had incidents similar to this. The only conditions necessary seem to be being in a relaxed state of "knowing" and to be unaware of the time at any point during the trip. This means not looking at a watch or listening to a radio where you might hear the time. Such "knowing" is an internal subjective awareness. Our society encourages us to pay attention to our objective external environment and to deny or ignore our internal intuitive environment. If something does not register on our five basic senses, we are taught, it is not "real." Did it seem strange in Chapter 2 that "a little voice" told the manifestor at the wine festival raffle to buy six more tickets? This ability to tune into our intuition can prove to be a highly useful resource. It gives us information that often is at odds with our intellect and reasoning and yet is very accurate.

> While picking up some fabric at a store I suddenly asked the owner as I was leaving if she knew of any good upholsterers. I had no idea why I asked the question except that I have an antique chair I've thought about upholstering for about ten years but have never had extra money to do it. The next day I saw my mother, who said she wanted to give me the money to upholster the chair. Wowee!

> Today during my noon walk, I started up Church Street from the corner of Main. I thought, "I wonder what I'll be led to that I need?" I kept walking and when I reached Hall's Card Shop I realized I should go to What an Interesting Bookstore. There I found the perfect book to help me with a personal problem I was wrestling with.

Perhaps not surprisingly, women mention this capacity more often than men in the group. Are we told as males not to trust anything that is illogical or subjective in origin? If so, we can learn to become aware of our own active intuition--those "hunches" that often turn out to be inspired. The intuitive feeling is subtle. Yet, as we have already seen, this subjective tool can be extremely valuable in the process of manifesting. Besides giving useful information, it can help one avoid discomfort and disappointment.

> I thought about taking some personal things home, since we would be emptying the boat soon. I thought I might need to take the dental floss home. I thought, "No, I have some at home." Well, when I was cleaning my teeth tonight, my dental floss ran out.

> When I was unloading the car I saw my sun hat, and my inner voice said I should take it. My rational voice said, "No, it's no good when it's really windy, and anyway, I have a visor to wear." Well, we had tremendous gusts of wind and within the first half hour my visor blew off into the water. Today we spent about three hours going very slowly in the hot sun. I could have used my sun hat. When will I ever listen?

> I tried many times to reach a client with whom I had scheduled a session. As I got up to go to the bathroom I had the thought, "Wait. She'll be calling in a few minutes." I didn't wait. She did call and I was unable to speak to her.

Not only does a kind of "inner voice" speak to us, but our bodies also send us messages. Again, the answers can be very helpful if we overcome our cultural belief that only the mind should make major decisions. In the next example, a woman has been agonizing whether to accept a job offer. Her mind has been encouraging her to do so, while her heart and body give her different messages.

I've been putting a lot of energy into trying to make a logical decision--asking the kids for their thoughts, making pros and cons lists myself. I've been obsessed with looking for the right answer. My body has been trying to give me the answer. I would feel sick when I thought about accepting the job, and a sense of relief would come over me when I'd think about turning it down. Instead of listening to my body about turning it down, I would try to justify the job because of the good pay, flexible hours, and convenient location.

When we run our lives using only logic, we limit ourselves and expose ourselves to much unnecessary discomfort. Notice that all the logical reasons given for taking the job are responses to external expectations. There is no mention of her intrinsic satisfaction or personal fulfillment. When we deny such useful sources of information as our bodies or our intuition, we deny a part of ourselves. And in so doing we deny a fuller, richer, and more joyful relationship with life.

Being Open to the Form It Comes In

It was the opening concert of the annual Mozart Festival. I loved classical music and my mother, girl friend and I would soon be sharing this beautiful music together. Unfortunately, as we approached the toll booth, I noticed a big sign saying CONCERT SOLD OUT. With great disappointment I pulled off to the side wondering what to do. My passengers were more disappointed for me than for themselves. It was a beautiful evening, and we drove into the mountains looking for a nice place to watch the sun set. Off one mountain road I noticed a large gathering of cars. Curious, I asked a passerby what was going on. She told me the Vermont Symphony Orchestra was holding an outdoor concert. We parked and walked over to the entrance looking to buy tickets. Because we had missed the opening number, the gatekeeper told us to forget the entrance fee. We strolled down to the front and had a wonderful free concert. Afterwards my mother took us to a nearby bar to buy us a drink. Within five minutes a pair of folksingers began singing right in front of our table. We were entertained with a second free concert.

This manifestor's heart was set on a concert that turned out to be sold out. However, there was much good will on the part of all the passengers, which was transferred to him. He gave up on the original goal and trusted they would have fun doing something together. In a word, he detached.

I had no conscious awareness of the possibility of another concert. Yet, somehow, I was guided to that mountain road with the concert. My goal was achieved. Only the form in which I had expected it to manifest was different. Through detaching from my original goal and form I was open to other possibilities of equal or even greater satisfaction.

We next return to an example discussed briefly earlier in the book. But now we explore it in more detail, so as to understand better the importance of being open to the form in which a desire is manifested. To try to control the form in which it comes limits the possibilities. How could anyone, for example, imagine ahead of time the following result?

For over a year I had been trying to manifest new colors in my living room studio. I researched the colors and patterns that would please and refresh me. It was a gradual process and I did not have the money to afford the redecoration. However, in my imagination I visualized this change about twice a month. I had confidence that some day it would happen. I had no idea when but I "knew" my time for change would be soon. I could taste it. One day a hose on my washing machine broke, flooding a good portion of the house, including the living room studio. An insurance check covered almost the entire cost of the redecoration.

It would be hard to anticipate the "accident" that led to the redecoration. Assuming one is honest, this is not something that one plans. Yet the goal was accomplished. Here is another example:

I had been told I was a good skier but I had never seen myself ski. One day I decided to see myself ski. I was clear with my intent. I let it go and just knew it would somehow come to me. Perhaps someone could film me. For the next couple of days I keep my eyes opened to see who would come along with a camera who would ski with me, but this did not happen.

The next time I went skiing, I was going up the chairlift and my intuition told me to ski down Nose Dive. I didn't want to do this because I just skied that slope and wanted to ski Hay Ride while the snow was still good. I decided to listen to my intuition. It was a cloudy day but as I was skiing the clouds opened up and the bright sun cast a perfect shadow directly in front of me just where I normally look when I ski. The shadow could not have been more perfectly placed! I could clearly see my style and this provided me with just the information I wanted. I learned from this incident that we get what we ask for but not always in the form we expect.

In another incident the same person had had a bad day shooting golf. His friend told him that a video of his game would show him exactly what he was doing wrong. He "put it out" that he wanted to see himself playing golf

72

and this included, but was not restricted to, a video recording. That night he had a lucid split-screen dream-- two images were next to each other. On the left he saw himself with the wrong swing. On the right he saw the perfect swing and could easily see the difference. "I now knew what I was doing wrong in my swing. I was tight in my shoulders." Once again this illustrates what happens when one does not limit the possibilities of how the desire manifests itself. Who would expect the answer to come in a dream?

> My husband wanted a home computer but we didn't have the money at the time. I said, "We'll manifest it." The next day he came home with a memo from the college administration saying they knew how important computers are to their faculty and that they were granting interest free loans to purchase computers. This was like out of the blue.

> For years I had wanted a nice warm winter fur hat where it circles around the top of the head. Although this is rather sad, things do come to you even if you never know how they will come to you. My husband's father died a couple of months ago. A hat, like I just described, was given to me by his wife. It means a lot to me because it was his. Again it proves things come to you but you don't know how or when.

> After graduating, I was in a high-pressure job. After several months I did not know what to do except I knew I needed a <u>break</u>. Soon after, when

on the boat, I <u>broke</u> my big toe and had to limit my activity for a whole week so it could heal.

My iron was completely plugged up. I could have thrown it out, but cleaning it was my preference. But how? I trusted that an answer would come. Eleven o'clock that night on the way to bed I took a vitamin. I opened the cupboard door and on the door was an article on how to clean things, including plugged up irons. I was amazed but then said, "Of course."

I needed some Christmas paper to wrap my niece's gift but didn't have time to shop for it. There on top of the dumpster was some great wrapping paper someone else was throwing out. Things come to you when you want them.

These manifestations did not involve extensive focusing or using visualization and affirmation tools. Instead, these manifestations came from a trust or certainty that an answer to the desire would manifest. The time from desire to manifestation was sometimes quite lengthy--years in the case of the fur hat. In other cases, such as the incident of the dirty iron, it was very brief. The manifestors <u>allowed</u> the process to bring the expected result. "Putting it out" was one phrase used. Also, almost all the manifestors realized that everything does come to us, even though we do not know what form will bring it.

One amusing incident concerns a car tape player eject button. The eject button would stick and would not dislodge the tape.

One of the manifestors and myself had decided to do a joint "miracle" healing of this apparatus. We knew from other manifestors that it was possible to "heal" mechanical objects. We would visualize every day or even more frequently the ejector button working correctly. We had very elaborate visualizations, even seeing ourselves as little mechanics working on the release mechanism. For several weeks we did this, without success. One day while driving a friend to his home, I mentioned the problem. He just happened to have his tool kit with him, since he needed to do some work on his own home. While I was driving he took the tape recorder apart, squirted some oil on it, replaced it and it has worked quite well ever since. The whole process took perhaps ten minutes. It was so easy compared to what my friend and I had determined was the proper way to fix this apparatus. This was a valuable lesson for both of us not to decide the way the apparatus would be fixed. By determining this ahead of time we were limiting ourselves to just one possibility and making it a far more difficult task to complete than was warranted.

This case again illustrates how we can limit ourselves by determining the form of a desired goal. There is great abundance and if we are not too attached to a specific form, we may actually receive something even more meaningful--or more easily--than we expected. We may find that we are getting what we really want rather than what we think we want.

The final example involves a teacher who wanted to be recognized for her abilities by winning a special teaching award.

> I so wanted to win this teaching award. I didn't get it--but I received a call from the professor who had evaluated my presentation for the award. He introduced himself as the person who had had the pleasure of sitting in my class. He was calling because I had made such a tremendous impact on him. My talk was on death, dying, and grief. His sister in law was dealing with her father's death, and he had wanted to know how to help her. This was a wonderful affirmation of my attempt to teach students how to cope with loss. I realized I had not failed in my effort to be an effective teacher. I was able to let go of my sense of failure. I don't need to win an award to know that my teaching does make a difference in people's lives.

As we close, let's review what we have covered in this chapter about successful manifestations. First, develop clarity in your goals. Second, choose a method of visualization or affirmation that feels comfortable for you. Third, after doing the visualization or affirmation, release or detach from the outcome. Do not try to force it. Trust that what is highest and best for you with regard to this goal is now in process. And, finally, do not try to determine ahead of time what form the outcome should take. Be open to all possibilities.

As in previous chapters, we close by encouraging you to experiment. If something we recommend here does not seem right for you, try something else. There are a great many ways to become a successful manifestor, and a small group of people manifesting for two years has not covered all the possibilities. Above all, learn to listen to that inner sense, follow it, and watch for the results.

CHAPTER 4

WHEN THE ENERGY STARTS TO FLOW

In the first three chapters, we have discussed a variety of successful short-term manifestations--parking places, enjoyable experiences, and desired objects. We have also given you glimpses portions of larger and more elaborate manifestations to illustrate the essential concepts of detachment and trust. In this chapter we will focus on only one person's manifestation. The desired goal grows out of a series of issues most of us have asked ourselves at some point in our lives. What is our real life's work? Do we deserve to have a job that uses our talents and creative skills while financially supporting us? Is there a job out there that can bring us greater satisfaction than our present situation and do we have the courage to go for it?

This is the story of a woman who, at first, felt she had to settle for a job she hated simply to support herself. Within a short time on the job, however, she decided that she was going to find a way to do what she loved and be paid for it. She then set about attracting a job that would use her special skills and talents and give her much greater satisfaction.

This account includes many of the concepts, techniques, and processes we have already discussed. It also introduces material we will discuss later in the book.

The first section of this chapter is this manifestor's own account, presented almost verbatim. The second portion is a discussion of parts of her story, highlighting the aspects that are particularly relevant to the manifestation process. When you have reached that point, we encourage you to return to the original manifestation and reread it, appreciating its detail and its significance. It is a remarkable example of what is possible when you define a goal clearly and commit yourself to achieve that goal.

Manifesting the Perfect Job

I started to work as a bookkeeper because I desperately needed work. I had been out of work for six months and my personal life was not good. I was coming from a very scarce place in my life. I took the first job I could get. I had no background in bookkeeping and no desire to be a bookkeeper.

I took the job and did it adequately, but it was really a situation where my best skills were not being used. There was no joy for me in the position. It was real drudgery. I went to work every day and did what I had to do. There was discomfort because I was doing a job from day to day that was about numbers. I would sit at my desk and work at a computer and punch numbers. I hated this work. I was there for a year and a half. Three months into the job I knew I needed something else but how could I go about finding a new job?

I came to a place where I had to do something. For quite awhile I went through the paper and went to functions that might help me obtain a new job. But nothing was happening. I realize now, looking back, that doing bookkeeping was not why I was there.

Fortunately, while I was on my job, a lot of healing was going on. I was building my self-esteem, which at the time was really low. That came from working with people who liked me as a person and did not identify me with my job. I got involved with a lot of creative things while I was there, and it really started energy flowing. I started making jewelry and having shows for people. The organization was designing a new building to move into and asked me to be the interior designer. I was doing a lot of things that had nothing to do with my job, but it was having a positive impact on my self-esteem.

That led me to visualize what could come next. I was emotionally at a point where I was able to realize there would be something next. I began doing affirmations about three months before I left the organization. Walking on my way to work, I would talk to myself and say out loud what it was I wanted. It could be anything from, "I deserve to be loved," "I am loveable" to "I am bright and intelligent" and "I need to be at a job where I use my skills." I didn't think a lot about it. I just said whatever I needed to say that day. I also had a small chalkboard on my apartment door. I reminded myself by writing affirmations on the chalkboard so when I would leave the apartment I would remember them. It could be the word "abundance" or "breathe," in times when I was feeling tight, or "Keep breathing."

I recited these affirmations for about 15 minutes each day on my way to work. People looked at me strangely because I was talking to myself. This made me smile. I did this for a couple of months. Going to work was a visualization exercise for the future; a sort of affirmation for the positive things in my life at the moment and to come. Coming home after work was sort of a "letting go." I would let go of the day, let go of the stress and negativity. Sometimes I would feel bad about myself and my job, and I wanted to change that by letting go.

I didn't have a specific job in mind for the visualization. But I did have some thoughts and feelings about it. I wanted to be in a job where I had some autonomy. I wanted to be using my communication skills. I knew I was a good organizer. I wanted to use the skills I had, and I wanted things to come to me more easily.

Most of my life I had chosen things where I had to work really hard and struggle. I was not interested in doing that any longer. I wanted to find a good fit. I wanted to utilize some of my natural talents and skills. People would tell me, "You are so good at talking to people," and "you are so articulate or sensitive." People had been telling me these things all my life, but it never helped me feel secure or created a real level of abundance. I really wanted that to happen. But I didn't know how. I didn't know what to visualize to make that happen. I didn't know what job to visualize. I kept affirming, "I will find something where I can use these skills. And I don't know right now what that looks like and what the job name is. But I want to do that." I also had a time limit because I knew the organization was moving. If they moved I knew I was not going to be able to go with them because of transportation problems. I did not own nor could I afford to own a car. So what I wanted to happen needed to happen soon. I knew that. There wasn't a sense of urgency but there definitely was a timeline. I couldn't take the next three years to work on this process. It had to happen. I think having those time lines worked well for me. In my heart of hearts I knew it would happen. I felt really confident that something would come along. Whatever was going to come, I needed it to come soon. I didn't know if it would be the perfect thing but I knew something would come.

I started applying for positions and going for interviews but things weren't clicking terribly well. I saw one ad in the paper I liked but I didn't have the qualifications for it. So I didn't apply for it because I didn't have the confidence and feared that I would fail to get it. A friend of mine who had seen the same ad said I would be perfect for this job and should just apply for it. I said, "No, I don't have the qualifications."

She said, "Well, I know the woman. She is a really nice woman and you can talk to her and get your foot in the door."

So I made the phone call and, by chance, there were two women with the same last name. I got the wrong woman. She had no idea what I was talking about, and she was kind of cold and rude to me. I called my friend and she told me I got the wrong woman, and to try again. I really didn't want to. I was resisting the whole process. I was afraid--afraid I would be rejected. I didn't want to get my hopes up because I would be disappointed. But my friend encouraged me to call again, and I did. This time I got the right woman. But when I reached her, she was on the way out the door and was brief with me and not very friendly. So I decided to not apply for the job and let it go and did not think about it again.

About a week later on a Sunday morning, I was with my friend in a laundromat I never go to. The woman who was the director of this program was there. My friend said, "That's her. Let me introduce you." So we were introduced over some washing machines. She was in her raggedy clothes and I was in my raggedy clothes. We talked about a lot of different things. I asked her to tell me about the job, and she did. I knew by the description she gave me I could do it. But I didn't have the skills on paper. She asked if I had applied for the job, and I said no. She encouraged me to apply, saying, "I want to see your resume." She seemed to like me, and that gave me more confidence to apply. I went home that night and wrote a cover letter. It had to be on her desk the next day. Usually when I do cover letters it takes days to write them. I had it on her desk by noon the next day.

Then I let it go. Now she has got it, I felt, so let it happen. She has told me since that had she just seen my resume, she probably would not have called me in for an interview because I did not have the qualifications on paper. But because she met and liked me, that made a big difference.

So I went in for an interview. It was a natural and easy connection; it was just "meant to be." (I hate to use that cliche.) She told me there were three final candidates, one of whom was me. But they were strongly leaning towards this other woman, and I knew that. So I thought, Well, I will go through this exercise for the practice, but I probably won't get the job. When I went into the interview--and I have never acted this way before--I acted as if I already had the job. I basically told them what I was going to do in that position. I had an agenda and gave it to them. I never would do that in an interview. Never. They were just that impressed. I had let go of my expectations. I decided I was just going to be myself and be creative and I don't care what they think about it because I am not that invested in it anyway. I let it go. Because of that my confidence level was up. It felt right. It was easy. I felt comfortable. And because of that everything moved. They were so impressed they offered me the job on the spot. They never even finished the interviews with the other people.

I remember leaving thinking, "I don't believe I got this job. This job pays $10,000 more than the job I have now." I knew I needed to make more than I was making, but I wasn't attached to the money. I was able to let go. I thought I would make money in stages. That I would make that kind of money in a chunk was surprising to me. It was so easy. It was not a difficult process. They hardly asked me any questions. It just fit. They felt it and I felt it. The job has just been incredible. I've gotten everything in this position I could hope for. I have the autonomy. I have a lot of responsibility. There is a lot of creative work. I'm going to meetings, talking to people, organizing events, and hiring and supervising people. I'm doing all the things I've always wanted to do. Because I love it and it is natural, I'm doing a great job. And the affirmations are coming from them.

Three months into the job, they have upgraded the position because I am doing more and working at a higher level than they had expected. I really enjoy what I am doing. I like going to work every day and doing it. I like people telling me I am doing a great job and to keep it up. "What can we do to help you?" they keep asking me. It is empowering. In most of my former jobs I had to advocate heavily for myself to get raises and recognition. It was a real struggle. In this job, there are more affirmations than I can deal with some days. Some days I can barely stand to hear one more compliment. And yet it helps me work more effectively. It is just an incredible situation.

It just feels like it was meant to be. Affirming that it was going to happen helped to get me prepared for it happening, to recognize it happening and to trust. I trusted that the universe would provide. I gave it some clear direction as to what I wanted and then stepped back and let it happen.

Many times opportunities come up and you try to make it happen. There is a kind of holding on to something. You say to yourself that this has to work. I felt like I had to get out of my own way; to step aside and take my best shot and then let everything else fall into place and to trust it would work. I let go and it worked for me.

Manifesting a Car

There is an interesting sideline to this story. One of the reasons this woman had to leave the first organization before they moved was that she did not have a car. However, her new job would require her to travel around the state; thus she would have an even greater need for a car. She had very little time and almost no money to make this very necessary purchase. Her personal account is, once again, both informative and inspirational.

I have not had a car in ten years. I sold my car to travel. I have never been in a situation financially to put a down payment on a car. I have always had to depend on other people for transportation.

So when the organization moved, I knew I would not have a job because I could not get out to their new location. I knew I needed a car. I knew that if everything was going to fall into place I needed to help it along. One of the things I needed was independence. I needed to be able to find a job that was not within walking distance.

I decided to do a jewelry show to raise money for a car. And I had a figure in mind. I wanted to raise $1500. But I thought that was too much to ask for. Maybe I could raise a thousand. I thought a thousand would be okay. But in the back of my mind was $1500.

For about three or four months I went home after work and made jewelry. I thought I would love to have 200 to 250 pieces for the show. I knew that was absurd, but if I could do that it would be a big show. After a month I had ten pieces. I really had to work hard. I felt good and stressed out. I work well under pressure, so I just was pumping them out.

About a week before the show I sat down to count the pieces and I had 250. Before this, I had no idea how many I had. So I had the show and it was a huge success. I invited 100 people and about 80 came. There was incredible abundance. People brought me gifts and flowers. There was food. There was dancing. People bought jewelry as if it were on sale. I spent the whole time talking and wrapping. I never left the room. People were buying stuff like crazy. It was a very positive experience emotionally because it was a wonderful affirmation about my art work and about support and love and friendship in the community.

I had a vision of what I wanted the show to look like and it surpassed it. It was better than what I had imagined. People were loving of me. It was just a very full day. I was exhausted. For days after the show I didn't count the money. I was burnt out. But after a few days I sat down and put things in order and started cleaning up and I realized I had made 1500 dollars to the penny. During the sale I didn't even think about the amount. I was just in the moment and selling things like crazy. I never thought about it.

And I went a week later and put a down payment on a car. I needed to have a car for the new job. The timing was perfect. They wouldn't have given me the job if I didn't have a car. I got the job before my show, and it was an act of faith I would have enough money to buy the car. I told them I was buying a car, but I didn't know how I was going to at the time I accepted the job. I was hoping the show would provide that for me. I knew the job would pay me enough to meet the car payments. It all happened at the same time. The car came one week before I started my new job.

There was a lot of letting go and trusting it was going to happen. I gave it my best shot and then stepped back. And it has worked.

So I have a car and a job that I love and I'm making more money than I've made in 15 years. It is easy and keeps building on itself. It is very challenging in a positive way. This is something I can build on.

It's really interesting how energy works. I feel good about what I am doing and I feel positive about myself. So people respond to me differently. Now when I tell people what I do, it feels like a truer representation of who I am. I feel good about who I am in the world. Everything starts to flow. When you are doing what is right, it all starts to click and fits into place. It is not that you don't have challenges, but you have the tools to meet the challenges. I have a lot more faith in abundance and that things really can happen. There is a certain bit of magic there. I don't know how we create it or how the universe creates it for us. But it is wonderful.

Here I am driving through southern Vermont with the beautiful snow on the mountains and I'm in my new car listening to classical music and I'm saying to myself, "I get paid to do this. I get paid to talk to people and to drive in my car in this beautiful countryside." I don't punch a clock. When I go to meet with people, they pick up on the positive energy. It is almost as if the words don't matter. I'm happy doing what I am doing. I believe in the program and I'm so comfortable that people want to be a part of it. They ask, "What can we do? How can we make this work?" If I approached them bummed out, maybe they wouldn't want to be part of the program regardless of how they themselves felt. It is amazing how positive energy creates more and more positive energy. It works upon itself.

Commentary on Manifesting the Perfect Job

This is a very human story. Though it has a happy ending, this woman experienced considerable self doubt and fear at various points during the manifestation. She literally hated her job. When you are really hurting it is hard to see a way out. Often everything seems to be going wrong at the same time. A significant personal relationship had just broken up, she had been out of work for six months, and all she could find was a "real drudgery position." She recognized she was coming from a "scarce place" in her life. However, beggars can't be choosers. The pain finally got to the point where she "had to do something" but she didn't know what to do. How often it is that things have to get really bad before we will take the action that will correct the situation! Even a bad work situation can seem tolerable if one is afraid of the alternatives. Better the unpleasantness of the known than the risk of the unknown, even if taking such a risk might result in great rewards of opportunity and happiness.

It is worth noting that she did take advantage of what resources were available to her. Her world was not one of total scarcity. She identified with colleagues who supported her, and she involved herself in creative activities that had nothing to do with her job but were helpful in building her self-esteem.

She also began doing, on a regular basis, a series of affirmations. What was important was the regularity and commitment to a process of using affirmations rather than the particular wording of the affirmations themselves. She said "whatever I needed to say that day." It could have been anything that was needed at that moment--anything! She was in charge of her process and she was working from a point of present time. She did not "think a lot about it" and simply worked the routine into her daily life. She said out loud to herself what she _wanted_ rather than only asking for what she thought was "realistic" or what she thought she could have.

She talked "positively" on the way to work and was not particularly concerned about what others thought of her. Coming home was "a sort of letting go" of the "pain," "stress and negativity" she experienced on the job. She was forgiving herself for being in the work situation she was in and not carrying home with her a victim mindset. It would have been so easy to fall into the "poor-little-me" consciousness. But by releasing the stress on her way home, she was open to creating a new, more supportive environment for herself. So often we remain mentally mired in the negative circumstances of our present situation and do not fully free ourselves to commit to and create a new situation.

Note that she "didn't have a specific job in mind for the visualization," though she "did have some thoughts and feelings about it." There were certain attributes that she knew should be included in any job, such as a feeling of autonomy and the use of her communication skills. She wanted a "fit" between the needs of the job and the personal skills she felt she would bring to it. A job had to be more than just a paycheck. She wanted to be paid and supported for doing what she loved to do.

"Knowing" was also part of this manifestation. "I came to the realization it would happen," she says. "In my heart of hearts I <u>knew</u> it." She knew she was not going to move with the organization. "I <u>knew</u> something would come."

At this point, we have an element of trust and detachment. She had not identified a specific job--all she had were "thoughts and feelings" about it. So she put out her job desire to the universe and then watched for the unfolding. On the surface, it looked like the job manifestation was not even working. She mixed up who to contact and called the wrong person. Then she decided not even to apply for the job. She "<u>let it go</u> and did not think about it again." As she learned later, had she submitted her resume to the director at the start of the application process, she likely would have been rejected because she didn't have the required skills on paper. It is often difficult for us to anticipate how best the unfolding will take place.

Who could have anticipated a "chance" meeting at a laundromat to which she never went? This was a crucial introduction, since her resume was weak. Was this really a chance meeting? We leave that to the reader's speculation.

During the several phases of the interview process, notice how frequently she refers to the concept of "letting it go," which we have referred to as detachment. After she left her resume on the director's desk, she "let it go." During the interview process she decided she would be herself and not "care what they think about it because I wasn't that invested in it." "I let go of my expectations," she says.

In detaching, it can be helpful to develop the attitude that you don't have to have something. Neediness or attachment can actually get in the way. By viewing the interview as an "exercise for practice" and pretending she already had the job, she circumvented this condition of neediness. Learning what "tricks" work for you can be extremely helpful, particularly in an emotionally charged situation, such as a job interview. By having to win you might actually increase your chances of losing.

When she held a jewelry sale to raise money for a car, she says, "During the sale I didn't even think about the amount" of money she had to raise. "I was just in the moment." Even after the show "for days I didn't count the

93

money." As she says, "There was a lot of letting go and trusting it was going to happen."

Finally, it is worth calling attention to her observations about the working of energy. Because she loves what she is doing she feels good about herself. And when you feel good about yourself, she says, "everything starts to flow." Situations and experiences seem to fall into place effortlessly. Her energy, in turn, brings her more creative opportunities and the people she meets "pick up" on her energy. "It is almost as if words don't matter." People pick up on her positive energy and want to become a part of that same process, which in turn promotes her work goals as well as their own. "I'm so happy doing what I am doing and people pick up on that and want to be a part of it." The energy and enthusiasm she puts out get amplified, are mirrored by others back to her, and create more and more productivity and satisfaction for her and probably everyone involved with her.

She doesn't understand how it all works, and it isn't really necessary to understand the process to know that it does work. "There is a certain bit of magic there. I don't know how we create it or how the universe creates it for us. But it is wonderful!"

CHAPTER 5

WHY WE DON'T ALWAYS SEEM TO MANIFEST WHAT WE DESIRE

One manifestor and his wife were visiting the fairgrounds with a friend from New York. While having a bite to eat at a picnic table, the friend noticed sea gulls circling overhead. "I hate sea gulls," she remarked. "I'm always afraid they're going to poop on me." Less than a minute later, a large load landed in her hair. A few days later, this same woman was back in New York jogging. Within a few minutes a sea gull dropped a load, hitting her squarely in the chest.

Surely she didn't desire either experience. In fact, she wasn't even consciously thinking about the sea gulls the second time. Yet in some way she attracted both experiences.

Throughout this book we have been asserting that we are always manifesting, whether or not we are conscious of our participation. Our beliefs are constantly creating outward reflections in the physical world, and there is no external censor saying, "Oh, she doesn't really mean or want this." What we experience in physical form is exactly what we expect or believe.

What belief, we can ask, is leading to the undesirable manifestation? To ask this question presupposes that we are willing to accept responsibility for an experience, such as being"bombed" by sea gulls, that we interpret as unpleasant. It is much easier to blame it on the sea gulls, on a cruel act of fate or, if all else fails, on the government for not getting rid of the dirty nuisances.

Perhaps, at first, we don't immediately recognize how our belief could be manifested in the droppings of a sea gull. How does the principle of continuous manifesting explain that I haven't won Megabucks yet, that I haven't found the perfect mate or job, and that my health could stand much improvement? There are days when I don't get a convenient parking place when I definitely need one. These are things I consciously desire. Most of us have similar desires. Yet our experiences (or projections) do not always seem to match them. We all have times when it seems hard to manifest anything and our lives appear to be caught up in a whirlwind of events that seem out of control.

This chapter will examine some of the more challenging and frustrating moments we experienced as students of the manifestation process. It would be untrue and very unhelpful to give you the impression that learning to work effectively with this process was always simple. It was not. It was a learning experience that included frustration and even some perceived failures.

Yet few members of the group found these moments of disappointment totally discouraging. In fact, often greater learning and enjoyment came from our so-called failures than from our successes.

Our Unrecognized Beliefs Around Scarcity

We begin with an undramatic manifestation--an incident all of us have probably experienced at some point in our daily lives. Yet, this example illustrates many principles that can help us understand why we might not manifest some of our larger desires, such as creating more money, a fulfilling love life, or better health.

It was one of those days where there was not enough time to do everything I had to do. Everything seemed to be coming at once. Just as I seemed to get things lined up, my wife gave me four more things to do. She keeps telling me I better hurry because there is so much to do. So I started to do these errands with my car. No sooner do I start than this little old man pulls out in front of me going two miles per hour and I can't get by him. The light is green but he slows down so it turns red. I am getting more and more frustrated. But then I decide to sit on the sideline and watch the frustration instead of letting it run me. I take the position of an observer. As I am driving along, all I am doing is noticing. I have never seen so many hindrances going from point A to point B. Just as this little old man pulls into a gas station, this big dump truck pulls out in front of me. The intersection is backed up three lights' worth and I'm watching this all unfold.

I ended up an hour late. I could have walked faster. I began to recognize that I had a belief around scarcity of time. It was like a lesson plan in disguise. I flowed with the energy for the lesson. I was fascinated to watch it and see what happened.

It would have been easy for this person to get more and more frustrated and angry with events and to blame some external agent or act for this misfortune. There were plenty of choices--the little old man, the dump truck driver, his wife, God, or even the government, which did not provide a four-lane highway or more synchronized traffic lights.

This manifestor knew, however, that everything he experienced in his life was related to some belief of his. He accepted responsibility for this frustrating series of events (perhaps reluctantly) and sought the belief behind the manifestation. He looked to his own experience for his teaching. By simply observing his own experience, he worked back to the belief or beliefs that created the experience. By becoming fascinated with the events as they unfolded, and by not judging them, he was able to identify the belief creating the circumstances. Thus, ultimately, he could give himself the choice to change that belief or at least to give it less energy or power over him. On that particular day he had a strong belief in the scarcity of time.

Whatever belief we give energy to manifests. It is not simply the holding of a belief that leads to its manifestation but the energy we give to it. By worrying or getting frustrated about not having enough time to complete all his errands, he was giving energy to the concept of time scarcity. Over and over he was saying, "There is not enough time," and, like the good mirror life is of our beliefs, he found himself having experiences that reflected that belief.

To have the choice of changing the belief--or the amount of energy placed on it--it is first useful to identify the kind of belief that might create such circumstances. This requires taking responsibility for one's circumstances and often doing a bit of detective work. A good detective is open minded, and indeed it is easiest to discover our causal beliefs in a nonjudgmental atmosphere of open and honest searching.

Here's another example. For several years, a manifestor enjoyed excellent health all winter but then came down with a serious cold in late winter or early spring. "When I realized that I created this cold in response to the belief that it is not 'normal' to go through an entire winter without at least one cold, I was able to break that unpleasant cycle."

Assuming responsibility for his spring cold helped him to recognize various sources for his beliefs.

Everyone around him seemed to get at least one cold during the winter. What made him different? Fear would tell him that he was setting himself up for a very heavy and disabling cold when it finally did come.

> I felt I had used up some imaginary and unspecified amount of good health, which I would have to pay for at some time in the coming year. For me I had to deal with a specific belief around scarcity of good health as well as a more general belief that I must "earn" or balance some good experiences with some not-so-good ones. Though he had passed away many years earlier, I could still hear my father's voice: "Into every life some rain must fall," and "Experiencing hardship builds character."

One member of the manifestation group felt that the process of recording desired manifestations was a form of bragging. "It makes me feel like I am boasting and saying, 'Look what I can do,' which I feel is counterproductive. Perhaps if I just stay in awe of the things happening that I have thought about, that is a respectful place to be with manifesting." She seemed to be saying that in our culture it is not okay to be prosperous and also feel good about it. If on one hand there is a strong perception that there is not enough to go around, that there is scarcity, then it may be inappropriate to want too much for oneself. If, on the other hand, one lives in a world of abundance, then we can all celebrate our good fortune.

Several members of the manifestation group were dealing with another form of belief in scarcity, a lack of work or money. One manifestor felt "harried and desperate about money." He was, he said, "doing work I don't like doing and I don't know how to change it. I have a lot of fear." He was afraid to leave a job he detested and paid poorly; yet he made no effort to project a new work goal. "I think I've avoided setting meaningful goals to avoid disappointment--the fear being that if I don't have a goal, no one can prevent my achieving it. Nothing ventured, nothing lost."

Not only was he coming from a belief in scarcity of meaningful work that would financially support him, but he lacked a belief in himself to manifest what he needed. His own fears about his past "failures" and the current poor economic conditions had almost paralyzed him. Yet, he was also aware that he could choose to move beyond his self-doubts, fears, and limiting beliefs.

> It is so difficult to trust myself that there will be a way to pay my bills if I go after a job that really turns me on. It is a continual process of letting go the fear and old beliefs that you have to do what you don't want or believe in to survive. We know in our hearts this is not true. Yet, we keep listening to our minds, fears, and culture and keep overruling our heart and spirit that tells us it is not true. I know that it is time for me to trust that more.

A part of him, what he defined as his "heart and spirit," was leading him more and more in the direction of trusting in himself and in the abundance of the universe.

Several months later he was beginning to formulate answers to his own fears. "You can learn to be more conscious of what your beliefs are. You can make friends with your fears. You can listen to them instead of running away from them." He recognized that for himself, "Changing beliefs is a slow process. It takes time to change who you are. It takes practice to be a good tennis player. Expecting immediate results only creates frustration. Why not enjoy the process?"

By focusing on what you do not have, you attract more of what you do not have. We hold onto present circumstances, such as a job we detest, because we don't believe in a natural abundance in the universe to provide us with the appropriate things at the appropriate times. To believe that we must struggle to attain the desired things in our lives may also imply a belief in scarcity-- for if we believed those desired things were abundant, we would be more likely to believe it was easy to obtain them.

It is a challenge not to be affected by the environment around us. If television news or newspapers are constantly reminding us of bad times for others or warning us of bad times ahead, we are likely to internalize those beliefs and thus manifest them for ourselves.

There has been increasing talk of the national economic slump. Being self-employed and easily stressed makes it difficult not to worry. I have a hard time foreseeing financial success while the people and papers claim economic problems. I know my fear of economic tight wallets causes me more trouble than the actual economy itself. And I realize if work stays slow it could be proof to move on or change. Realizing I could have been causing my own lack of customers got me to focus on reversing that. I have allowed whatever happens to happen, feeling secure enough even if it did stay slow . . . . These past few days have brought business galore. It feels like tourist season.

This statement illustrates several things. First, this person accepts responsibility for his own circumstances; he realizes he is not fated to be wedded to a belief in a poor economic outcome that may be present in the larger society. Second, this manifestor is willing to consider moving to a new job or location if conditions do not improve. He is open to new avenues through which abundance can be manifested. Finally, he is able to allow "whatever happens to happen," trusting that an appropriate experience will follow. Many of us in similar circumstances would worry, obsess, and want to control and direct circumstances where our livelihood was at stake. He was able to detach and allow for abundance.

Attachment Is Believing
You Cannot Create What You Want

It seems cruel that just when we most need or want something, we are actually creating the opposite condition. A strong feeling of "neediness" keeps our good from us. At the end of the year, we sent a questionnaire to members of the manifestation group. We asked them which factors seemed to facilitate and which factors seemed to detract from their ability to manifest. A common observation was that detachment and confidence were important facilitators. Feeling "needy" and "having to be in control" were inhibitors.

> I was most successful when I was open to the outcome and didn't have a preconceived idea about the outcome. I had the most trouble manifesting when I desperately wanted or thought I knew what I wanted or what the outcome should be. When I feel busy and need it the most is when I don't seem able to manifest.

> I'm least powerful as a manifestor when I'm attached and feeling I just have to have it! At that time I'm coming from a place of insecurity and fear.

> I'm most powerful as a manifestor when I feel good about myself, relaxed, playful and loving. When I can let go and let the universe take care of it. When I am depressed, feeling out of control and angry and feel the need to control

people and the environment is when I have difficulty.

My greatest successes are when I am feeling strong and confident, and where the manifested element isn't desperately needed.

A street artist noted that when he worried about how to attract customers and felt needy about money was when he had difficulty making sales. "When I start the day slow I lose all confidence in myself and the possibility for having a good day. Believing that I am a good artist and not thinking about the need to make money seems to lead to more sales."

An art teacher and a practicing painter noted, "It is important for me to be energetically connected to my art as expression and not as a money maker. When I hold tightly to my paintings and feel I have to sell them to live, I have trouble selling them. When I am doing new paintings, my old ones start to sell." When her focus detaches from the need to make money and shifts to that of creating new works of art, the paintings naturally start to sell.

Attachment is a special form of a belief. It is a belief that you cannot create what you want. If you are attached to having it, you fear that you may not get it. This again goes back to a belief in scarcity, which in turn may stem from a lack of faith in your ability to create what you want and need. The key question to ask yourself is whether it is all right with you if the desired object or experience doesn't manifest.

When you are attached, you are afraid. You may be giving power to the beliefs such as "I am not worthy to receive" or "Scarcity is everywhere." Focusing on the belief in scarcity will bring scarcity to you. However, if it doesn't matter whether it comes or not, you are giving support to the belief in abundance or you might be recognizing that there are many ways your goals can be fulfilled. Perhaps even something better will come your way than what you have already asked for. You are relaxed, confident, and trusting in the outcome of your desire.

So you don't win Megabucks. Money may come in some other form. Or perhaps you attain a feeling of security and safety in your life, which was what you really wanted in the first place. You thought having a lot of money would achieve this.

Gentle Changes in Beliefs
for the Semi-skeptical Manifestor

A patient had an advanced case of cancer of the lymph nodes. The doctor who had been treating him had exhausted all standard treatments. The patient did not want to die. He heard of a new experimental drug called Krebiozen and begged his doctor to let him try it. Reluctantly his doctor gave him a dose of the drug on a Friday. On Monday, the doctor examined his patient and was amazed to report that "the tumors had melted like snowballs on a hot stove." Within ten days the patient left the hospital cancer free.

About two months after leaving the hospital, the patient came across some articles that said the experimental drug Krebiozen had been tested and found to be ineffective in treating his form of cancer. He suffered a relapse and was readmitted to the hospital. This time the doctor decided to try an experiment. He told his patient that the drug was effective if given in the proper concentration. This was not true, of course, but the patient was excited to try a dose with the supposed new concentration.

The results were dramatic. The patient was once again quickly free of symptoms and he left the hospital. Within about two months, the American Medical Association announced that a nationwide study found the drug worthless. This time the patient was shattered. The cancer blossomed anew and he died two days later.

This case is one of the most famous examples, cited in many books and articles, of the power of our conscious minds to heal our bodies. However, few of us are likely to respond so dramatically to external information. Many scientific "wonder discoveries" have failed or have limited benefits, and we are aware of the need for testing over long periods of time for side effects as well as for favorable consequences. Our scientific and medical sophistication often makes us more skeptical, and this skepticism can actually work to our detriment for healing. Since there are few real miracle medical cures, most of the medical profession is reluctant to acknowledge the relationship between healing and consciousness. As patients, we are too sophisticated to be tricked the way this patient was with the new experimental drug. Is there still a way to work with or bypass our beliefs about our limited power to heal ourselves?

We believe there is. Let's return for a moment to Paul, the group member with the painful tennis elbow. His profession required him to work continually with "objective" scientific principles and to view the body as just another machine. When his body was uncomfortable, he sought some external substance (medication) or some intrusive action (surgery) to get the machine back in working order. He felt he could not discount some fifty years of indoctrination overnight, so he looked for a less dramatic and more gentle way of dealing with his beliefs about healing.

> The pain around the elbow was most pronounced when I played tennis, and I had for years tried a variety of remedies to reduce the discomfort. For example, I tried to use a two-handed backhand, which felt awkward to me but did not produce as much discomfort as my preferred one-arm backhand. I also wore an arm brace. However, the only real cure was many days of rest between matches. During actual play. I learned to endure the pain.

One day my family doctor recommended a sports medicine specialist, who in turn gave me some limited advice about exercising and ice packs and recommended a medication I had not tried before. Given my belief in the power of medication and the newness of the drug, I left feeling I had found a wonder drug. Within a few hours I felt noticeable relief. It was supposed to take at least several days to have much effect. For some reason I knew I had found my own miracle drug. I invested tremendous power in the drug. I visualized it encircling my elbow with healing white energy. I began to limit my doses to half doses and even pretend doses. That is, I would pretend to take the pill and would still do a healing visualization. There was no regular pattern to how I used the medication. I followed a kind of intuitive route as far as the use of medication and ice packs. It didn't seem to matter what I did. The condition steadily improved. Although I experience very minor discomfort, a kind of stiffness or mild soreness several hours after playing, this is extremely minor when compared with a time I thought I might have to give up playing altogether. In any case there is probably a residual part of myself that is still a bit skeptical, and perhaps this small part is still reflected in the discomfort in my body.

We mention this experience for those of you who may find it difficult to make dramatic changes in your beliefs, such as the Krebiozan case, but who can <u>suspend your disbeliefs</u> for a while and experiment with them.

Often, developing this new belief in self-healing does not involve new learning as much as it involves <u>unlearning</u> or temporarily putting aside "negative" conditioning that claims these abilities are not "real."

> Since I loved taking a pill for this condition, why not enhance the power of the drug so that half the medication had twice the power? Or perhaps an ice pack alone would be all that would be needed if I had not played any matches but just helped coach my son (even though the play would be just as strenuous).

Beliefs can be temporarily put on a shelf to allow for a new opening. The negative belief can be de-energized and a new belief energized.

> I would take half the medication and visualize a full-strength effect, thus allowing my old belief in medication to have its satisfaction while I strove to energize the new belief in my own power to heal. I didn't give up my belief in the medication. In fact, in the beginning I actually enhanced it. But over time I put my energy in a different place, in my own capacity to heal myself. I was the experiment and the experimenter, and I enjoyed the challenge of playing with my own beliefs. I did not deny them but loosened them from their hold on my consciousness and, in so doing, they had less and less control over me. More and more, I was able to choose which beliefs I wished to give energy to while still acknowledging the presence of my old beliefs. Gradually like very old habits, which

they were, they were loosened and then replaced with new beliefs. I then had choices. I could still take the medications, but I knew I was not dependent on them, either.

Further Hints for Changing Outmoded Beliefs

Our environment is a powerful shaper and reinforcer of our beliefs. Becoming more aware of the environment and how it influences us can give us choices about how to respond to that environment or even whether we wish to create a different, more supportive environment.

What messages do you receive through the interactions you have with your present environment? For example, do you find that the people you associate with regularly come from a place of abundance and creativity or from a place of scarcity and victimization? Do you listen regularly to news stories about violence, scarcity, and fear? You can support yourself in changing your personal beliefs by avoiding people and experiences that feed you "negative messages" and seeking out people and experiences that support your new beliefs.

This was one of the major functions of the manifestation group. Through the support we received from each other, we were able to go beyond our existing beliefs of limitation. For example, one member was experimenting with time. She was able to drive from her home thirty miles away to the group meeting in a period of time that seemed humanly impossible given our present beliefs around time and matter. Yet she found time very fluid, and she encouraged us to experiment using techniques she found useful. We did, and we were able to replicate her results for ourselves. The support we gave each other allowed us to go beyond the self-imposed limitations of our beliefs.

Another member of the group was successful in fixing her broken car radio through visualization and conscious intent, a manifestation that will be detailed in a later chapter. Again, this information gave the rest of us the courage and support to try this on our own appliances.

We hadn't thought of such an experiment ourselves, and we were surprised that it could be successful. Using only conscious intent, many of us found we were capable of fixing car engines, leaking pipes, and rototillers that hadn't worked for some time. Again, a supportive environment allowed us to go beyond our own self-imposed, limiting beliefs of what was possible.

Look at your larger environment--your neighborhood, community, and government. Are the organizations with which you are involved promoting beliefs that favor victimization and scarcity? Do you feel the energy you spend in such groups is productive when you look at them from a self-empowerment perspective?

As previously mentioned, many of us found that watching television news--with so much stress on societal crisis, negativity, and scarcity--was not supportive of our beliefs. Politics, too, seemed to reinforce a belief in helplessness in the face of large geopolitical forces and events beyond our control. Crime, war, massive financial deficits, mass starvation, and natural disasters were nightly fare. You may find this is not the mental environment you want, either.

It may also be worth exploring your own personal history environment for unresolved issues that may be undermining your self-worth. Once they become aware of them, it is possible for some people simply to change limiting beliefs without having to understand the origin of those beliefs in their family. Others find it useful to recognize their source in past family experiences. One person, for example, traced his lack of belief in his own creative power to his parents' highly critical and authoritative way of raising him.

A self-loving attitude is obviously a great asset in successful manifesting. In naming the circumstances that seemed to contribute to successful manifesting, members often mentioned feelings of confidence and love and the presence of a kind of calm, centered energy.

> I am most effective when I'm relaxed, centered, in control and have more time. Mind and emotions are synchronized with each other and I feel more love and more ability to visualize.

I feel most powerful when I am relaxed, confident, happy and connected to my heart space or inner self.

When I love myself and my esteem is high is when I am most powerful. Also when I am centered, and grounded mentally, emotionally, physically and spiritually. I am working with complete trust and unconditional love. I am detached and know without reservation that all is well. I am truly present but out of my own way.

When I feel balanced, open, and centered, I can feel the energy charging through my system. My energy level is very crucial for manifesting.

Centered energy seems to include elements of calmness, assurance and confidence. There is an implied acceptance of oneself and others. Energy flows freely in such a state. On the other hand, when your energy is low it is hard to manifest. Everything becomes a chore, and self-doubts and feelings of neediness can reduce effectiveness.

When in such states of low energy--and all of us spend some time in such a place--it may be helpful to realize that there is a natural ebb and flow of energy in life. There is a natural balance of active and passive or receptive energy. When manifesting, you are actively putting out energy. But you need to allow time for the results to manifest. Action is balanced by receptiveness to the desired outcome.

In our culture, which stresses "doing" over "being," we often feel uncomfortable in a low-energy or low-activity state. Rather than resisting or denying such energy, you can just acknowledge its presence and allow it to pass through you, trusting that it will shift again. Denying its presence only gives it more energy and inhibits its flow in and out of you.

It is always helpful to nurture yourself in whatever way you have found reinforces feelings of value and self-worth. "I find that walking by a lake during a beautiful sunset or buying a treasured piece of music or eating a special favorite food helps the energy to flow through more rapidly," says one manifestor. We recommend that you appreciate the abundance of what you have in your life rather than focusing on what is missing or absent. We all have our own unique way or ways of nurturing ourselves. Find your ways of expressing self-love and practice them. To do so is not a selfish act. Through greater love and appreciation of yourself, you will be more effective in supporting and assisting others with their needs.

Conclusion

The manifestation process is rarely a quick fix or cure-all for every desire you have. It is a tool to include in your repertory of ways to enrich your life through self-empowerment. As you try manifesting, and perhaps experience what seems to be failure, do not be judgmental of yourself. Recognize that many of the beliefs that seem to stand in the way of what you desire have been accumulating for many years. These familiar beliefs and attitudes provide a kind of comfort and security, no matter how much we may wish to change them.

A few lucky people can kick their habits overnight with a sharp act of will. You probably know some former cigarette smokers who successfully went cold turkey and others who took years to relinquish the habit. Unwanted beliefs internalized within us and reinforced by our culture follow a similar process; you may need time to loosen and then replace them with healthier and more desirable beliefs. For many of us the whittling down and "fake-it-till-you-make-it" approach can be quite effective.

You can choose to bludgeon your self-imposed limitations, or you can gently work to replace them with new attitudes and behaviors. As we have been saying, identify those beliefs you want to change, be clear on what you want to replace them with, and then experiment to find which process of change is most comfortable for you.

CHAPTER 6

MANIFESTATION AS A WAY OF LIFE

After nearly a year of participating in the manifestation project, we asked the members to reflect on how their involvement in the group and working with the concept of manifestation had changed their lives. As they looked back over the year when they first began consciously manifesting their desires, what, if anything, was different from the way they were manifesting now? Their answers frequently began by referring to the earliest exercises around locating parking places.

When I first started out by manifesting parking places, it was kind of a test. Now I don't even test that since it has happened so often. When I go downtown, even to places where people never find a spot, I know I'll find one even closer.

I don't do a lot of heavy-duty manifesting. When I am pulling into a parking lot, someone will be coming out and I get a parking place like no problem. I don't write them down any longer. I just don't worry about it.

I believe I have a lot of experiences where things work out to my advantage but during

117

which I don't consciously manifest something. It's almost as if the universe is realizing what I need and is sending it to me.

These statements illustrate a process most manifestors experienced--that manifesting became more and more effortless. In the beginning, manifestors tended to test the limits of their beliefs; they were often amazed when their stated desires materialized. They were quite deliberate, active, and conscious about the process. A person wanted a parking place in a certain location at a certain time, or they wanted a particular article of clothing at a specific price. They had some very definite details in mind.

Gradually, most manifestors found such effort was unnecessary and could even impede the manifestation if they did not detach from the outcome. One manifestor reported she was "not so goal oriented" and was "more open to the outcome of what is there." Another manifestor noted that at first she stressed "specifics" or the "form" in which the manifestation came. "I find the more I let go of form, the more it works." And still another manifestor reported that she was "less controlling and demanding and more accepting of circumstances."

Letting go of form and outcome is another way of saying they had more trust in their ability to create what they needed. There was a greater trust in the purpose of all experiences without needing to be fully conscious of the process. As one manifestor said: "I don't have proof. I don't need it. It is the healthiest way to operate. I just trust it is so." Another manifestor said he had a "greater conviction that the universe is a friendly place and it works to bring about the highest and best."

> When things really look bad in my life I trust things will have a good outcome, even when I can't see it. Internal battles get shorter and shorter.

In one case a manifestor had been subjected to being harassed and stalked by her former husband. She had hoped to write a story about this incident to raise the consciousness of the public and the state legislators, who were debating a bill to make this a crime. She felt inadequate as a writer but had a strong desire to write something so that others might be protected from what she had experienced. As it turned out, through a series of "chance" events, a writer from the Associated Press wanted to do her story, which turned out to be very satisfying for her. Her main goal was to help others by publicizing this problem, and she attracted someone who could facilitate her desire.

Others, too, found a "silver lining" in all experiences. Because they took more self-responsibility, they had less anger and judgment and often desired to use their less-pleasant experiences to assist others.

Another manifestor said that he had "a greater sensitivity to improbable events that seem to support my goals." There was an openness and receptiveness to what was coming even, if it might not seem to make sense in terms of the desired goals. Somehow he "knew" what was presently happening was part of a "plan" to bring him what he needed and desired, but he was not able to see the plan in advance. He trusted, was open to receiving, and "tuned in to whatever was out there."

During their year of practice, most manifestors had become quite confident in their ability to create. They had become increasingly convinced that they were creating all the experiences in their lives.

> I now understand that I create my own reality, and that my attitude dictates whether a given event is negative or positive. Energy attracts like energy; therefore when I am sending out positive energy, I receive positive energy.

> This year I have experienced many instances of thinking or wishing for something and then experiencing a lead or some other direct event or conversation that created the very thing I wanted. It's clear our energy does create the reality we experience.

> By recording my manifestations I become the observer and I can reflect on them and become more convinced and also more appreciative. Otherwise I just might chalk it up to luck, coincidence, or happenstance and let it be. The examination of this process is wonderful.

For most of the manifestors, journaling was not necessary after a period of time to convince themselves of their own creative power. For a few of us, however, it was helpful to draw attention on a regular basis to all the manifested incidents in our lives. The log itself, kept for months, was data for those of us who were more skeptical and who needed a tangible reminder of the validity of this process.

Finally, although manifesting parking places no longer required much effort or even interest, there was still unmistakable joy and fascination with the process.

> Life flows more smoothly. Large and small goals are coming to me easier and with less stress. I feel like I don't have to put boundaries on my goals. Working on goals is more <u>fun</u>; the process makes life more interesting and helps me feel more connected to the universe.

> I listen more to my heart now and not my ego. I understand more who I am. I don't have any big revelation moments. It's all the small ones that make the difference. You let your love and light shine through to the harried sales clerk and transform her day as well as yours. You put out the energy and it comes back. My life is deeper, richer, more spontaneous and has more serendipity.

> I'm more aware of and appreciative of the serendipitous events of life. And I'm more aware of the incidents that have been a part of

manifesting, whereas before I might have just called it fate. It has become a more amazing world!

It is more of a subconscious synchronicity than effort. I still do parking spaces. In the past few months I've been delighted by the "chance" meetings on the street of people I needed to contact or talk to or people who have come into my life who have had a profound effect on the way I view myself and the world. I know I've drawn these people to me and the larger manifestations such as new work, education, and home. I have been successful.

The manifestors have come away with a newfound appreciation of their own power to create in their lives. The experiences they have brought to themselves in their daily existence have become transformed in meaning. Life has become richer and more meaningful. Events they might once have dismissed as chance have taken on new significance. For manifestors, there is no such thing as a "chance" meeting on the street. They make connections between events even they do not at first have a full rational understanding of their significance.

And it is not just the major manifested experiences, such as that new job or home, that seem so astounding. As one manifestor says, it is the myriad of "all the small ones that make the difference." It is that consciousness or awareness of the meaning behind many ordinary events and daily experiences that gives our existence a magical quality. In the next section, we will look at some examples of this ordinary magic.

Notions of Manifesting

The word <u>notion</u> captures the effortless way manifestors kept discovering meaning in the events that unfolded in their lives. Notion can imply a "vague thought," "an inclination," or a "whim," according to Webster's dictionary. Sometimes we were surprised by what we manifested because our intentions were such fleeting thoughts or desires that we were unaware of them. We then had to work back from the manifestation itself to discover the thought behind it. This process helped us recognize some of the subtle ways in which our thoughts manifest in the physical world.

Of course, something that manifests may not seem to have been the recipient of any energy. Yet, over time, you may realize you have been giving energy to a belief which, in turn, eventually has crystallized into physical form.

As autumn approached, one participant remembered that in past years it was the time when his allergies began to act up. He noticed other people blowing their noses and talking about their allergies. Weather reports gave the pollen count daily. Medications were frequently advertised in the media. He found more and more reinforcement for the belief that "it was that time of year" when allergy sufferers give themselves permission to feel miserable. Not surprisingly, this belief supported years of past allergic suffering for him.

But most members of the manifestation group recorded experiences that were overwhelmingly positive. Many of these events were minor, but they speak for themselves.

Some time ago I put out to the universe that I wanted to know more about Word Perfect's graphics and style's capabilities. I wanted to take a workshop but not have to pay for it I simply could not afford it. I put that out in a fleeting request, nothing major. I just visualized the information I needed. Well, last week I got a call from someone named Don M. saying he had written a course on Desktop Publishing with Word Perfect and was going to teach a free dry run of it. Would I be interested? I said, "Sure," and took it on Tuesday. It turned out to be a full-day workshop. I learned a lot about graphics styles--just what I wanted to know!

I put it out to the universe that I needed $100 for a trip to Hampton Beach within three days. I put it out and let it go. The whole process took only a few seconds. I had said to the universe I don't care where it comes from. I could almost feel it coming back to me. I didn't think about it. The next day my parents came by and gave me my birthday present early. It was $100. I had had no conscious contact with them, although they knew

I was going away for a few days. In previous years they gave me clothes and sometimes $25. I had never gotten $100 from them.

I had to come up with $150 for a pair of glasses. Just then a friend called me and asked me to type up his Master's thesis for $150. They paid me in advance. It was a veritable miracle and came just when I needed it. But it wasn't anything I was visualizing or trying to manifest very consciously. <u>I just knew that it would be there and I didn't worry about it.</u> There was far too much else going on in my life.

I was running short of cash and needed some work. I remember putting out a prayer; <u>a little concentrated wish</u> that I wanted more work to come to me before I did anything or went anywhere. What came in the mail that day but some requested editing. It was only a couple of hours' worth of work, but I will say it was pretty darn fast. It couldn't have been handier. It came right to my door. I didn't even have to make a phone call.

These manifestations, which all involve the desire for money, were quite effortless. There was not a great deal of ego invested in any of them. The manifestors "put it out" to the universe, went on with their daily lives, and trusted that some unseen force or action was working on their behalf. It was a "little concentrated wish," a "fleeting request," or something that they "knew" would occur. The manifestors were relatively detached and, for the most part, were unconcerned about the "when" and the "how" of manifesting these desires.

Here are some more examples that show how often the answers we seek come to us quite easily if we are alert to receive them.

Today I realized I manifested a green magic marker. On Friday, while at work, I was using a red magic marker and also had a yellow one. I wanted a green one for a certain chore. I thought to myself they probably didn't have green in the office and didn't even bother to ask. Today at noon a co-worker had been sitting at my desk. When he returned to his own office, he took everything with him except a green magic marker.

Several times in my kitchen I have thought wouldn't it be nice to have a little radio. I really should go and buy a little radio because my stereo is too far away to hear while I am in the kitchen. Then a few weeks ago my fiancee showed up and said, "Oh, by the way, I bought you this little radio." I never thought about manifesting. I didn't make that connection until now. Maybe we work too hard at things that are simple.

I was thinking about my plugged-up iron today. Should I throw it out or clean it? Clean it is my preference. But how? I trust an answer will come. At eleven o'clock that evening on my way to bed I took a vitamin. When I opened the cupboard door on the door was an article on how to clean things, plugged-up irons included. I was amazed, and then I said, "but of course."

I was tossing out summer catalogues and I saw a cotton violet dress that I've been admiring for two years in the Spiegel catalogue. It was $68 and I didn't want to pay that. I thought <u>wouldn't it be great if</u> I could get this dress for $25? Then I thought, Spiegel never puts their prices that low. Today a sale catalogue came from Spiegel and I flipped through it quickly. I saw the dress on sale for $24.90.

During a meeting a man walked by and accidentally stepped on my foot. He said, "I'm sorry, and for stepping on your feet I'll give you these," and he dropped some nail clippers into my lap. Just that morning my mother had asked me for some nail clippers. I didn't have any but <u>thought to myself that we do need some clippers.</u> It was just a passing thought. I could hardly believe it when they landed in my lap.

After I left my job I continued to get calls at the old business phone and my business partner would call me with messages. I thought, <u>Wouldn't it be nice if</u> I could get my old telephone number, and I thought about it for a month. Yesterday in particular I thought about it. Today my former business partner said he was moving and asked if I wanted my business number back.

Before I left Burlington, I had wanted to organize an art show for females who had survived childhood sexual abuse. When I moved down here, I really wanted to do something in that arena. <u>I put that out to the universe.</u> I thought about it and kept my mind open to things. Two weeks ago I saw an ad in a weekly newspaper: "Wanted: Volunteers to help organize an art show of survivor art." I couldn't believe it. I called right away and met with a wonderful person who is also a recent transplant.

As time approached for me to go back to work I asked the universe what I should do about my car as it is standard and shifts like a tank and I knew it would kill my painful arm <u>I no more put the thought out</u> when my daughter called to offer the easy-driving car and we have swapped cars ever since, enabling me to work.

There were long lines at all the Grand Union checkouts. It looked like fifteen minutes of waiting at the least. I said, <u>I will manifest a new register opening up and I will be first in line.</u> I went over to grab a newspaper to bide my time. No sooner had I opened the paper when a woman came up to me and said, "I am making a new line and you can come over here if you like."

The person in the last manifestation was quite detached, and had even picked up a newspaper to read while waiting. He went on to tell me that in his previous experience with lines of waiting people, when a new line opened up everyone would rush over. In this case the check-out lady had to walk over to the end of one of several long lines and pick him out to tell him she was opening a new line. He did end up being first in line.

So many of these "ordinary" manifestations were quite effortless, accompanied by an intent or a mild desire--"Wouldn't it be nice if. . . ." In some cases, such as with the green magic marker, the manifestor logically concluded that there weren't any in the office. Yet the desire was registered and perhaps the logical deduction acted to release and detach the desire and thus make the manifestation possible.

Events such as these occur regularly but go unnoticed or are passed off as coincidence. By becoming more aware and appreciative of them, you give more energy to such occurrences and thus encourage still more such "little magical miracles," as we like to call them. Begin to look for these occurrences, expect them to appear, and you will find them. You will enjoy a richer, more exciting and more empowered life.

Living in the Flow

During the summer, Todd and I would get together at his home in the country to work on the manifestation book you are reading. We lived about thirty minutes' driving time apart. His home was situated in a very peaceful and bucolic setting, and there we found we could be very productive.

We wanted to be flexible in our meeting times to allow for other events in our busy lives. After all, it <u>was</u> the summer. Rather than fix regular meetings, we decided to intuitively connect with one another when we "felt" it was appropriate. As a result, the times of writing and discussion seemed to follow a natural process of unfolding. We found that when we called each other to discuss the book or decide on a meeting time, almost always it "fit" with the other's schedule. When one of us was busy with family or other work matters, the other was often also busy. Our lives and the book project seemed to have a similar flow of energy.

We decided we wanted to tune into this flow and accept where we were in it without becoming frustrated if our expectations were not being met. At times the chapters seemed to move very quickly; at other times we were unable to produce any material for several weeks. Although we did become somewhat frustrated when things slowed down, we tried to recognize the natural ebb and flow of this project and to accept wherever we were without judging ourselves or the process. We enjoyed an intuitive satisfaction and peace when we were able to flow with the natural current or energy of the project.

I found that even my time of arrival at Todd's home always seemed to be perfect when we both were able to trust the flow of events. At times I would arrive considerably later than I had promised--which turned out to be perfect for Todd, since he had a task that took him longer to complete than he had anticipated. On one occasion I "seemed" to arrive early. I was feeling stressed and out of balance, and the time I spent quietly sitting alone actually facilitated our work when he was able to join me.

I liked to think of each of us as a river of energy, which in turn was flowing as part of a larger river of energy in a general direction. Our work together on the book represented streams of energy intertwined with the broader energy currents of our lives. We could choose to flow with those energies or try to force a particular pace or direction to our work. It seemed much more comfortable when we could let go and flow <u>with</u> the larger river of energy.

This was not always an easy "letting go," since both of us were used to a certain level of organization and structure in our lives. Meeting goals and deadlines provided reassuring evidence to ourselves of our productivity.

The process is subtle and requires an inner trust and a tuning inward to pick up intuitive directions. You can use outward events to monitor whether you are in the main flow of the current or are trying to "row upstream." When you are moving against the current, you may feel out of balance; events do not happen effortlessly and easily. Life may seem difficult and full of obstacles.

Several members of the manifestation group recognized this process and its value for their own lives.

When I calm myself and follow my intuition things happen just right. When I think everything through, I get out of touch with the flow of the universe. I can tell the difference and get back into the flow. We have these little voices that give us ideas. Wouldn't it be fun to do this or that? We need to listen to them because that leads us to manifest what we want.

I don't feel rushed or in a panic to find a job like I did last year. I do feel as if it will come to me. I have to trust my own gut instincts. When the career counseling class was filled, I realized I so often want to rely on other people's opinions for me. If I had been in her class, I would again have been asking her and the classmates to help me decide. This way I am forced to be more in tune with myself and more open to what the universe brings me. The other evening I was feeling fairly receptive to life and open, and that evening another job popped out of the paper at me!

I find myself experiencing much more flow than trying. I feel less in control but I am okay about it. I have a lot more trust than I used to have. There is something about "inner knowing." You don't have to convince anyone. It just is.

Learning to "tune in" to ourselves is an alien process for many of us. In the second example, we have a person who continues to seek external criteria for a job instead of looking within for guidance. Rather than feeling frustrated that she did not get into a class she hoped would give her answers, she saw instead an opportunity for her to seek her own answers, which seemed consistent with her energy flow. She could have become upset and perhaps tried to force her way into the class, or gotten very discouraged and simply given up. She had a choice--to resist the natural unfolding of events or to go with them and ask herself how to benefit from the experience.

When our manifestors began to observe what they were creating and to experiment by following those "little voices," "gut instincts" or "inner knowing," their lives seemed to flow more smoothly.

> I needed to lighten my class load and drop chemistry but I knew my advisor would not understand my situation since I had been out of school for almost twenty years. I thought getting some personal counseling first might make it easier to see him. Instead, I was notified for some reason that my advisors had changed. I got a very compassionate woman who gave me support and guidance. I took a replacement course that allowed me to talk out a lot of stress. I switched from a day to an evening course in another case. Somehow I knew it was perfect that I started out in the day course. The day course prepared me for the evening course. Throughout this whole process of switching courses and times and advisors, there was a gut part of me that said, Do this or that. It is a "knowledge" of knowing what you are supposed to do. And when you do follow this intuitive feeling, it gets incredibly validated. I need some

surgery now. Part of me, an intuitive knowing, says it is okay. I trust in my relationship to my higher power.

Here was a student with many decisions to make. She felt uncomfortable in certain classes and with certain people and had to "intuit" her way in a relatively new environment, having been out of school for so many years. While she was listening to this inner part of herself, she was also testing its validity, which made it easier and easier to both recognize it and to follow its guidance. She was creating harmony and flow with the larger current of energy which, in turn, was guiding and preparing her for her new career.

This last example on flow shows how little effort is needed. The manifestor only needed to have a clear intention and to listen to his intuition.

Each year in the fall, the Jericho Congregational Church has a chicken pie supper as a fund raiser. This tradition has been going on for just under 100 years, and is very popular with the local community. The tickets go on sale about a month before the dinner, and are usually sold out in a couple of days. Because it is so popular and the only advertising is by word of mouth, I have my computer remind me about six weeks ahead of the dinner's date.

This year, when the message on my computer appeared, I noted my intention to attend. But unlike past years I didn't put it on my TO DO list and forgot about it altogether.

Two days before the dinner, I was going hiking. My intuition said to take the back roads. This route takes me past Desso's, the store that sells the tickets, and as I approached, I thought I should stop to see if they had any tickets. Again my intuition interrupted and said to stop on the way back, which I did without giving it another thought. As I look back on this, I was surprised that my logic did not kick in with its usual advice, like, " It's too late, they are sold out." or "If they should have any tickets then stop now and not on the way back--someone else might get the last ones. "

It was late afternoon when the clerk at Desso's patiently told me they had been sold out of tickets for over three weeks. This conversation was overheard by the owner, who announced that someone had just turned some tickets back in about an hour ago. She asked me how many I wanted. I asked for four, as we usually ask another couple to go along. She only had two, which I took. I then gave her my name in case two more tickets came in.

Late Saturday morning, Desso's called with two more tickets. We called the people who usually go with us, but they were busy. Then my intuition said call Barry and Terri. They were available and delighted because they have never gone to the chicken pie supper.

That night as we finished dinner, Terri said that this dinner was perfect because just that morning she was dreaming of a turkey or chicken dinner with mashed potatoes, squash and homemade pie, which is just what she had. But she hadn't wanted to cook all that food. Now she had gotten all that she dreamed of, it was served to her, and she didn't even have to clean up. It all just seemed to flow.

Perhaps an analogy useful in understanding flow would be to consider what happens when a person who knows judo is attacked. Rather than putting up a wall of defense or attacking back with his own energy, he goes with the flow using the energy discharged in the attack to disable the attacker.

Another example might be a person in a canoe going down a rapids. The destination is chosen but the method and process of moving to that end is open and flexible. To move most quickly and effortlessly, it is easiest to move with the current guiding and directing the canoe around rocks and turbulence. In a similar fashion you can affirm a desire, such as two tickets to a dinner. You then trust and detach from the outcome. After the choice is made, you follow a river of life events, gently, always aware of that inner voice, that intuitive messenger that alerts you to stop at a store even though your logic tells you it is a waste of time.

Connectedness

How often have you thought of a friend and then, a few minutes later, gotten a call from them or run into them on the street? How does this happen? Is this simply a chance occurrence? Is there a network of telepathic energy connecting us all to each other? Is the bond comparable to that of a parent and child or husband and wife, where each seems to "sense" when the other has experienced some trauma or is in need of assistance even though physically separated?

For the members of the manifestation group, such "coincidences" were frequent. Unfortunately, we have no record of times when manifestors thought of someone and did <u>not</u> "connect" with them. That situation would have been more ordinary and would not be cause for comment. Perhaps the awareness or expectation itself would have hindered the connection. Or perhaps we do connect but are unconscious of the connection. There may be certain conditions having to do with detachment and focus that precede such occurrences. In so many of these incidents, the experiences themselves convinced these members that coincidence was not operating.

Here are some of these "coincidences." Are they manifestations? You judge for yourself.

I was trying to reach a work acquaintance I don't often talk to. The first time I tried to reach her, her line was busy. The second time I picked up the phone to call her, she was at that instant trying to call me because there was no dial tone. She never calls me. It was freaky that before I could dial her number she called me, and I picked it up even before the phone rang.

I was thinking about a friend who had moved to California because today was her birthday and I hadn't spoken with her for a long time. I haven't even thought about her, but today I did heavily. When I got home from work I lay down on the couch, the phone rang and it was my friend calling. Cool, eh Fred?

Yesterday I thought of a friend I hadn't seen or spoken to in four or five months. They moved out of the country and for some reason stopped talking to me. This morning at 7 A.M. the phone rang and I was awakened by this person, who wanted to resume our friendship.

All day long, I had this nagging feeling I should call a cousin I hadn't talked with for quite a few months. When I did call, I found out she had had a bad day and was so happy I had called. She had been feeling devastated and depressed. It was an incredible conversation--the best one I have ever had with her. We shared a lot of great stuff. The energy of the universe works in amazing ways.

I decided I would go see a business that has not advertised with us in three years. I was thinking about them a lot lately. On my way to this business, I stopped by the office and there on my desk was a message that they had called. They wanted to get an ad in the guide. Would I come see them right away? I love it when things connect!

I was thinking about Fred in Austria and hoping he was having a great time. I thought it would be nice to get a post card from him. When I went to the mail box at noon, there was a post card from Fred. I was really excited to get the card and to realize I had had a premonition.

I wanted to celebrate my parents' anniversary as a family. I thought wouldn't it be nice if my brother would fly up here so we all could be together. It seemed unlikely, given his family situation in Tennessee. Today my brother called and said, "What if I come to Vermont?" I couldn't believe it. I talk on the phone only about once every two to three years with him. And he has a free airline coupon that was going to waste, so it worked out great!

I got a message on my answering machine of a guy interested in buying my wood stove. I called him and left another message on his machine. He called me again and left a number to call that was just one digit off from the first phone number he had given me. I called that new number, but it was obviously the wrong number. I explained to the person I had reached that I had called in an attempt to reach someone else. This new guy said he and his wife were just talking about buying a wood stove that minute. I said, "I have an All-Nighter." And he said that was exactly what they had been trying to find, without success. He couldn't believe I was calling him the exact moment they were talking about buying a stove.

Are these manifestations in the way we have been discussing them? There is an effortlessness about them that in some cases is not even asking for a response. We may be thinking of someone but not necessarily asking them to call or contact us. Perhaps there is a wistful desire behind the thought that a physical connection be created. The situation with the brother coming to a family reunion unfolded even though the sister thought it logically unlikely. Once again we are reminded of the limitations logic imposes on our desires and creativity.

As evidence that some unseen network of energy connects us all, consider the seller of the stove and the person who had a "nagging feeling" to call her cousin. Empathic ties linked the family members despite the physical distance. And some kind of extraordinary communication linked up the needs of the woodstove buyer with the woodstove seller. Remember the many manifestations presented earlier of people who desired certain products and "just happened" to be in the right store at the right time and with the right price?

I needed someone to help me with my wreath making for my big November show. I ran into a neighbor at a barbecue who had taken a wreath making class from me in the past and came up to me and asked if I needed any help. After

140

agreeing, I ran into a second woman who said she was interested, too.

I have been working three jobs the past few weeks. Today I had a time conflict with two of those jobs, but I had no way of getting in touch with my boss to try and resolve the problem. For some strange reason he walked by one of the other places I was working. He just wanted to say "hello." I was able to tell him about my conflict and resolve it right then. The funny thing was that my boss has never just walked by to say hello. Everything worked out perfectly.

I had to get in touch with my music teacher before a 7 P.M. recital. I realized after I had missed her on the phone in the morning before going to work that it would be difficult to reach her. While having lunch downtown, I "ran into her" and got the information I needed.

A friend asked me if it would be possible to use the piano in St. Paul's Cathedral. I offered to speak to the head rector, whom I found out had moved to another parish. A short time later during a swim at the YMCA, I swam alongside the new rector and both of us got out of the water at the same time. We introduced ourselves to each other and I was able to ask whether my friend could use the piano, which was granted.

I had to reach this woman about a group boat trip tomorrow. I couldn't reach her by phone. While picking up some tickets to a future concert performance, I just happened to run into her coming out of the box office. The chances of this happening were very slim. A variation of a few seconds in time would have made the difference.

I was walking along Hampton Beach picking up sea shells. I came across a sand dollar with a chip. I said to myself, I want a whole sand dollar. Within ten minutes a woman came along the beach and came up to me and handed me a whole sand dollar. She told me this is very rare. Those were the only two sand dollars I saw during the four days I was there.

A friend of mine was in an important race and asked me to send him energy when he raced. I was in the library and working on a paper and forgot about the race. At about 11:30 I got this intense feeling he was running into problems and having a difficult time and needed energy. So I focused on his running by sending energy to him. Next time I talked to him, he told me of hitting a "wall" and felt extremely distraught and just thought there was no way he could finish. Later, he said this was around 11:30 or 11:40. He said right around that time he got a sudden spurt of energy and continued the race. At another time I did the same thing without telling him if or when I was sending the energy. He told me he got a spurt of energy right about the same time I had remembered sending it. This second time was more of an experiment to confirm the first incident.

At a breakfast stop I met a trucker who normally wouldn't stop there, but had just blown some tires. He asked me what I did. I mentioned that

I was involved in a new kind of healing process. He said his wife was very interested in alternative medicine and had various physical ailments. Although quite skeptical himself, he began talking about coming to see me in Vermont with his wife. He seemed to need to be there to talk to me. It is interesting how the universe adjusts schedules so that peoples' meetings can come about. The universe blew his tires to make him pull off. I don't know why I pulled off. I just did. I didn't think about doing it.

The first several incidents all relate to how we seem to draw the appropriate people to us when we have a need to contact them and when ordinary expected means of communication, such as the telephone, do not seem to be working. The way they unfold can't be controlled or planned. This is a challenging way for us to learn to trust and detach from a specific plan of action. How could a person plan to meet the boss at the other job or the minister at the pool or the contact at the box office or the music teacher while having lunch downtown?

One group member was interested in this matter of connectedness and did a little experiment of his own. He was an employee at a ski resort and was due to relieve another ski employee. Since he knew he was going to be late, he decided to send a telepathic message to another employee, who was also a friend, to do it for him. When he arrived late at his place of work, he found the regular guy had been relieved by his friend, just as he had projected. Later, on the way home, he decided to telepathically ask his friend to stop at a particular store and buy him a drink, which he also did.

For our final set of examples we will look at two cases of "connections" with non-humans. Unlike the previous incidents, which are quite common among our manifestors, we only have the following two examples.

> Pigeons had been running rampant in our garden and destroying it. I decided to "connect" with the pigeons and ask them to please go someplace else. Well, four weeks later the pigeons are gone. You can't imagine what this means to me, since for years every time I looked out the window or went out the door there they were looking at me. Did I really do this? I have no choice but to think I did, as there's no other explanation. Pigeons don't just up and leave when they've nested and roosted at a place for years.

> Our 38-year-old Shetland pony--blind, deaf, and suffering from arthritis--needed to be put out of her misery. I had been putting off putting her down. I began to communicate with her and tell her it would soon be her time. On Saturday when I fed her, I said with my mind, "Lady, if you would only die by yourself I wouldn't have to kill you but on Monday I'll have to make plans. It would be so nice if you would die naturally." I heard about a coming snowstorm and I wanted to do it before the snow came. I said to her, "If only you would die this morning." When I came home for lunch my

daughter said that when she had gone to feed Lady she found her dead in her stall and still warm. She showed no signs of struggle and was very peaceful. Yes, I do believe we communicated.

No doubt many readers have felt themselves communicating with their pets. But have they ever been able to verify that some communication was received and understood? These two examples are rare in our study, although there have been studies of communication with dolphins and plants. In this case the nature of the communication was some form of telepathy.

We close with an unusual example of communication that <u>may</u> have taken place between a human and a so-called inanimate object.

I was sitting on my porch with a friend. It was a beautiful sunny but cool day with a strong wind blowing. We were both tucked into our down-filled wicker chairs with light blankets, enjoying the day. I noticed an empty five-gallon pail blowing down my driveway toward the street. My driveway runs past the porch back to the barn, where I had left the bucket. I was so comfortable that I didn't want to get up to retrieve it. So I quickly visualized the bucket coming to me as it was on its way past. At that very moment the wind stopped and there was the bucket just ten feet from me in the middle of the driveway. Then the most amazing thing happened. The wind shifted direction by 90 degrees and blew the bucket right to my chair. I didn't even have to move in my chair to pick it up! Then the wind changed back to the direction it was blowing, and stayed that way for the rest of the day.I know because I watched it very closely. It certainly had my attention. Can manifesting be that simple?

Conclusion

We began with some everyday occurrences that we might be tempted to overlook and pass off as chance. We have ended with some rarer examples. We have suggested that some type of consciousness may connect all humans and perhaps humans and other living and non-living entities. There is increasing evidence of this phenomena in recent studies of quantum mechanics, particularly in the morphogenetic field theory of Rupert Sheldrake.

At this point we simply encourage you to consider these examples and look for them in your own life. Experiment. Stretch your own beliefs and see what is possible. Look for those "chance" meetings, phone conversations, and logically doubtful yet meaningful connections between events. Look for those events in your life today and you will see more of them tomorrow.

The large and very conscious manifestations, such as the healed elbow or ideal job, are wonderfully challenging and meaningful. But what the members of the manifestation group showed was that we can live day to day in a world bordering on magic. You have only to expand your consciousness, imagine possibilities, and <u>allow</u> for meaningful coincidences to unfold before your eyes. Or <u>play</u> with your life, as the person did who manifested the wind blowing a bucket to his side. Keep your belief in chance and fate, if it is necessary, but for a few moments each day consider the idea that some greater benevolent power, of which you are the guiding master, is available to enrich and give greater meaning and purpose to your life. Try not to take this process or yourself too seriously. Let it be fun! Become the experimenter in your own life and recognize and create your own connections for yourself. Become your own teacher. No one is better qualified to challenge you and to teach you about these phenomena than you yourself.

CHAPTER 7

ARE THERE LIMITS
TO WHAT WE CAN MANIFEST?

Alice laughed. "There's no use trying,"
she said. "One can't believe
impossible things."

"I dare say you haven't had much
practice," said the Queen. "When I
was your age, I always did it for half
an hour a day. Why sometimes I've
believed as many as six impossible
things before breakfast."

Lewis Carroll, Alice in Wonderland

Almost all members of the manifestation group
participated in creating parking places, material objects,
and a wide variety of experiences. Many also increased
their awareness of how flow contributes to greater harmony
in daily life, as discussed in the last chapter. A few people,
however, were able to manifest experiences that seemed
extraordinary. When we met regularly as a group, they

shared their experiences with the other members. Their accounts encouraged the rest of us and fired our enthusiasm to try these more challenging manifestations for ourselves. If one of us could do it, we felt, perhaps others could do it, too. This encouragement, of course, was one of the primary purposes of the manifestation group, and recounting these incidents is one of the primary purposes of this book. This is our message: We can do it, and so can you. If you are skeptical about these successes, don't just take our word for it; experience it for yourself--by expanding the limits of your own belief systems. Ultimately, we will ask at the conclusion of this chapter, whether there are any limits to what it is possible to manifest.

Self-Healing

"Thy faith hath made thee whole."
(Matthew: 9:22)

Have you ever tried to console someone who was suffering from a cold and have him say to you, "It's okay. I get a bad cold this time every year." What he seems to be saying is that he not only accepts the cold but that he actually expected to catch it! This example is not that different from the person in Chapter 1 who expected rain on his vacation. This is the energy he gives to the belief, which in turn attracts the bad weather or the illness.

149

One manifestor, reflecting on his process of health, reaffirms once again how we attract to ourselves what we believe:

> Frequently I have caught myself creating my own illnesses while feeling helpless to alter their course. When my sons come down with a bad cold or flu, I just assume that I will catch it sooner or later. Often they, in turn, catch it from their classmates and what they bring into the home is the same illness spreading throughout my classes and in the offices and buildings of my colleagues. At certain times of the year there seems to be a whole sickness mentality or consciousness in the community. It is a frequent topic of conversation. You can feel like an outsider if you haven't had or aren't coming down with the illness. It can almost seem inescapable.

One member of our group was particularly inspirational for many of us in resisting this fatalistic attitude. Her self-healing experiences were most inspirational for us during the Christmas season, when she had several concerts she did not want to miss. Neither her family nor her work environment was conducive to or supportive of good health at the time, and yet she was able to create good health for herself. She spent three weeks in constant close proximity to people with colds, including her husband. She committed herself not to succumb because of her upcoming singing concerts.

She described her method: "Every time I kissed family members with a cold or felt a possible symptom," she says, "I have said, I will not get this cold because I love my life, which is so full of wonderful activities, and I have a beautiful immune system that will boost up to ward off this virus."

Closer to Christmas, and even more concerts, she realized she was courting an illness. She was determined to be healthy for Christmas Eve, and she focused her energy in this direction. This had an interesting consequence for her after Christmas Eve passed.

> Everyone at work has had laryngitis with strep throat. I don't want it, as I am singing at two services on Christmas Eve. I decided I would try the immune system boost again. So every day I've been waking up and telling my body how wonderful it is and how I can't wait to get up and begin my day. In short, I have been sending love vibrations to my immune system.

> I did feel wonderful for both performances. But on Christmas day I felt terrible. I had a headache and sore throat that would not quit. On the night of the 25th, I realized what I had done. I had to demanifest my own script. I began movements to reverse the situation. On the 26th, I felt bad but better so I went to work, and today I am feeling perfectly well. Everyone else at work had to take time off and seek treatment with antibiotics. For the second time this year, I have prevented illness with my mind.

At the University of California at San Diego, sociologists have found that mortality drops by 35 percent the week before the Harvest Moon Festival, an important event in the Chinese calendar and a time of special reverence for the elderly. It rises by an equal amount the week after the festival. This suggests that people can postpone death to experience a favored occasion. The issue our manifestor faced was what to do after the concert had passed. She had to recharge her immune system. Though she was already ill, she experienced a very rapid healing compared with her colleagues who had the same illness.

Several weeks later, she did manifest an illness at the outbreak of the Gulf War. At that time she felt helpless to do anything about it. The events were too overwhelming.

> I was depressed all day long the day before and kept saying to myself, "I am sick at heart." By afternoon I had transferred that sickness to my body, as I felt sicker and sicker. I had to take the next day off. This was my first illness in many a moon. I had manifested health through boosting my immune system all year, and today I manifested illness. There is an illness in the world.

Four days later she was still very sick. While her friends, colleagues, and family members around her were sick, she was able to ward off illness. But something more distant, the flow of world events, was able to weaken her commitment and undoubtedly her immune system. Affirming verbally that she was sick, she gave the sickness physical form in her body. As she said several days later, "This has been a real bout, as it has been with the world."

Overcoming our internalized beliefs and expectations is part of the challenge. When these predispositions are reinforced by external authorities we have learned to obey, our goal of manifesting self-healing can be made even more difficult. Let's return once again to the manifestor with the sore tennis elbow. He recalls how his family physician first prescribed rest for at least six weeks, to be followed by only periodic play.

> This was very frustrating because I wanted to play more regularly. He had also told me about cortisone shots, but they would also only be temporary. After going to a sports medicine doctor, I felt I had done as much as could be done medically. All his suggestions centered about medical intervention with pain killers, elbow braces, ice packs, and exercises. I was led to believe it was a chronic condition that could be "managed" with proper treatment and rest. No one suggested that I might seek some mental cause and eventually cure the ailment.

At this point the patient was grateful to have found a better way to continue being athletically active, but he was also becoming frustrated with his inability to manifest what he really wanted to create--a cure for his sore elbow. He was surrounded by physicians who did not

153

offer him that alternative. Also, he knew of no one his age who had this condition and had cured it. He continued to search for that solution, "knowing" on some level that it must be possible.

Another manifestor experienced a major head injury when she was thrown from a horse. She had been given only a 30 percent chance of survival. When she did survive, her doctors were amazed but also advised her to accept her condition and the likelihood of long-term disability. She had always been very athletic, a tennis and volleyball player, and she was determined to regain her previous abilities despite her doctor's prognosis.

> In my mind I kept saying, I will be playing again soon. They said I probably would not be able to talk or walk. In the back of my mind I knew I had learned to talk, walk, and eat. I knew I could learn them again. I didn't want to go to the rehabilitation program. They were very compassionate but also very victim oriented. Everybody told me I should be happy and grateful to be alive. All I could see was that I couldn't hit the ball the way I had before. I have fully recovered. I have learned we can do whatever we put our minds to doing. If we can be more open the sky's the limit. I feel so much more now than I did before the accident that we all have tremendous mind power.

Another manifestor told us of her experiences following her birth in Oklahoma during a tornado, which hit the hospital.

Right after birth, the nurse took me running down a flight of stairs to the basement and dropped me and broke my back and the doctor said I would never walk again. My mother looked at the doctor and said, "Oh?" I was walking before I was a year old. When I was seven years old, I had polio and the doctors said I would never walk. My mother looked at the doctor and said, "Oh?" Within two years I was dancing. I became a professional dancer. My 90-year-old mother just broke her leg for the third time. The doctor told her she would be a vegetable. She looked at him and said, "Oh?" Mom started walking again after four months.

We do not have to look far to see where this manifestor picked up her own strong belief in her strength and abilities, and her determination to live life according to her own goals and intentions. Many belief systems, if not most, are family-based systems that are transmitted through many generations.

Both of these examples involve medical personnel who based their prognosis on previous experience or were trying to be compassionate by helping the patient accept her condition, so she would not be too disappointed if the disability persisted. Yet in doing so, they were almost condemning the patients to their disabilities.

In the second case, we were struck by the simplicity of the account of the mother who, for some reason, never doubted the healing outcome. Perhaps she was too naive to credit the doctors' experience and training and so did not see them as unquestioned authorities. Or perhaps whe simply felt no one is an unquestioned authority.

Another woman had been diagnosed as having a high risk of cancer of the cervix. She was told she would probably need a hysterectomy. This diagnosis frightened her because she was planning to start a family. Her response was to do a regular visualization exercise about being healthy by sending white light to the cervix. "I saw people as little maids dressed in black and white and cleaning the spots on my cervix." She also asked herself for a reason for why she had created this condition. "I thought it had to do with holding things in and not expressing myself and finding out who I am. I believe things happen to you because of holding things in that manifest physically."

Some manifestors were able to ask such meaningful questions with increasing ease the longer they were involved in the group, but this situation was unusual because of the seriousness of the illness. Moreover, this woman was not a member of the group; she was a friend of one of the members. Most people would probably find it difficult to accept responsibility for such a medical condition. It is one thing to wonder how our beliefs are preventing us from having a sunny vacation; it is another to accept responsibility for a precancerous condition that is likely to require a hysterectomy and eliminate the possibility of bearing a greatly desired child. For this woman, the visualization may have worked: the condition did disappear and she later became pregnant.

We close this section with a manifestation that used both traditional medical treatment and visualization techniques. On one hand, we cannot know which method was responsible for the healing. On the other hand, it did work--and for many of us who still feel a certain comfort with the medical model, it shows how one can take the best from two different approaches and maximize the probability of rapid healing. The manifestor herself had little doubt that the effectiveness lay in the <u>combination</u> of traditional and nontraditional methods. Again, this experience supports our premise that it is one's belief rather than one's method that produces the desired outcome.

> I was in a serious car accident where my car was stopped and I got rear ended by someone going 35 to 50 miles per hour. I had a bad neck injury from the snapping of my neck and was in considerable pain. I went to a doctor who took x-rays and said it was quite severe and would take several months of treatment. I studied the x-rays closely so I could understand the damage and see it clearly in my mind. I then asked the doctor to show me a normal x-ray so I could compare. I then put both pictures in my mind and brought the photos home in case my visualization got fuzzy or unclear.

I saw the doctor three times a week, got ultrasonic heat treatment, did exercises, and beefed this up with a massage. I used my own treatment of "powered-up" visualizations. I called on my spirit guide and his band of angels to assist. I often visualized many angels with their hands on my neck massaging all the out-of-place parts back into position and healing all the "bad" places with this wonderful warm white light emanating from their hands. I also did a healing tape with water and dolphins. Any time I "power up," I balance it with the same amount of gratefulness and thankfulness. The massage was also important for me, since it was just joy-type work. This balance is critical for me--active and resting "work" as a combination.

One month later, the x-rays revealed major improvement. The doctor noted how "remarkable" her healing was. He was treating several other people with the same injury as hers but they "had terrible neck and arm pain and many were crippled up and couldn't sleep."

What is striking about this last account is that the subject did not hesitate to use all the resources at her disposal to create a team of helpers: a traditional medical doctor, a masseuse who also did healing--even a group of visualized angels massaging her neck. "I needed a <u>team</u> who was kind and believed in healing." She took an active role in her own healing, which gave her confidence and ultimately brought success.

Manipulating Time

In his book <u>Unconditional Life,</u> Deepak Chopra tells of a small group of miners who were trapped underground after a massive cave-in. They realized that the air in the mine shaft would only last a few hours. Only one of the miners was wearing a wrist watch. In reporting the time, he decided to tell his comrades that an hour had passed after two hours had actually elapsed. Six days later, to the astonishment of the rescuers, all of them were found alive--all except one, the miner with the wristwatch. He could fool the other miners about the passage of time. But he could not fool himself.

In our group, manifestations around time were begun by just one member and spread like wildfire through the rest. This woman wanted to create more time for her personal life by being able to get more done in a given space of time. She also wanted to be more regular in arriving at her destinations.

She found when she wanted a class she was teaching to go faster, she could "contract time" and it would go faster. She could also expand time, doing housework that would normally take 2-1/2 hours of work in 1-1/2 hours. But her most popular manifestations among the group concerned her ability to get where she wanted to go at a particular time. For example, when she was not speeding and when she hit all green traffic lights, she had a fifteen-minute direct ride from her home to her place of work. Yet she found her time-expanding manifestation work allowed her to make two stops on the way to school and still arrive punctually in the same amount of time.

Time after time she projected arriving at a certain destination at a certain time, even when it would appear, given the route and speed limit, almost impossible. "I left home at six exactly and I planned to arrive at your house for our meeting at six forty-five without breaking the speed limit. I had manifested hitting all green lights. I did hit two red lights, but I pulled into your driveway at exactly six forty-five." Her example suggests again that we focus on the end result and not worry about how it is accomplished.

In working with time, there are different methods you can use. This manifestor did it "by visualizing arriving at a certain time and visualizing the time on my clock radio to slow down. I have done this ten times to the same destination this month and have gotten the same results every time."

Another manifestor decided to try this when he was late to a doctor's appointment.

> The first time I did this I had a doctor's appointment, a trip which normally took 35 minutes. I had only 23 minutes to get there. I wanted to be there at one o'clock but thought it would be okay to be five minutes late, so I focused on five minutes after one. I couldn't quite believe I could make up that much time. I

focused on seeing the clock in my mind saying just after one o'clock. I arrived there exactly at one o'clock. I don't know if this was a miss, since I had projected being a bit late. But I do know that I arrived at my ideal time. Something overrode my doubts about myself.

She tried it and told the group; he tried it and told the receptionist; she in turn tried it and told her son.

I told the doctor's receptionist with much enthusiasm about my experiment. She was intrigued. At my next visit she told me she had done the same thing herself very successfully. Moreover, she had told her son and he also was successful in projecting time of destination.

Just as this form of manifesting had spread within the group, it was now becoming popular outside the group as well. Here is a sample of other members' experiences:

I left my house late. I had less than fifteen minutes to get to the cafe to meet my friend. I was confronted with red light after red light. I envisioned I would arrive on the scene the same time as she did and it would not be important that the clock said exactly twelve o'clock. I walked in just as she got there, and amazingly the clock said noon.

I had a meeting with my friend, which always takes me 30 minutes to get to, but I had only 20 minutes to do it. So I really "pulled my car ahead." I did not look at a clock but did see myself getting to her house at the original time

I said I would. I did make it! I guess this is what she meant by expanding time. I don't know whether I expanded time or moved through space differently but something happened. It was an interesting experiment in "car pulling" or "time expanding."

At 8:30 I came to a closed bridge. I was supposed to be at the school at 9:00, and there were no nearby back-up routes. I turned around and started to fly. I got caught in traffic going into Essex and a very busy intersection at 8:45. Then I thought of calming down and concentrating on arriving at 8:57. I stopped looking at my watch. I stepped into the elementary school at 8:58.

I still try condensing time when I'm running late for something, and often it works. One time in particular the universe responded in an unusual way. I needed to be at a meeting at 11:30, and I visualized arriving in time all the way there. When I pulled into the lot and saw the clock it said 11:38. I was disappointed. My disappointment faded when I realized I was the first person to arrive. Everyone else was late, so my arrival time was still okay.

I had told my friend in New York I would drive into her driveway at exactly 8:03 which on my clock is 8 because it is set 3 minutes fast. This was leaving Burlington. At the rate I was going, there was no way I could make it by 8. I pictured the clock in my car to read 8:03 and I did it every hour of the trip. Sure enough, I pulled into her driveway at 8:03. There is no way possible I could have done that with the amount of time and distance I was at. I did drive a little faster but not enough to make a difference. I played with time in my mind and pictured getting there, and, sure enough, it happened.

Today my kids and I drove to Virginia. The kids asked me to manifest the time of arrival. I told them 5:28. I arrived exactly at 6 P.M. It occurred to me that I had told my sister in law that we would be there by 6:00 or I would call. Driving back to Vermont, I told the kids 5:28 again. I literally didn't look at the clock for about three hours, but when we turned into the parking lot, which is the destination I had projected for 5:28, my son said, "Look at the clock." I said, "Not until I park." When I did look, it said 5:28 exactly.

There are several observations worth noting about manifesting time of arrival. The first is that we sometimes get what we really want rather than what we think we want. The manifestor who wanted to arrive at his doctor's at one o'clock was unsure of his ability to manifest that time because it seemed a bit beyond what he could accept as possible. The person who was disappointed for not being on time was still the first one to arrive at the meeting, which was essentially her goal. Not being late and not keeping others waiting was more important than being at the meeting at a specific time.

Not looking at the clock, relaxing during the trip, and being confident of the outcome seems helpful. A sense of lightness and detachment combined with a clear focus or picture of the time of arrival seems to work for many. It is important not to look at a clock and not to keep checking your progress. Needing to check your progress is an indication of doubt, and putting energy on the doubt will manifest this lack of faith as the failure to arrive at the desired time. One of the most detailed accounts of time projection was recorded by a manifestor when driving from his home to his job, a trip that normally took at least fifty minutes. In this instance, he had only forty minutes to reach his destination by ten minutes to eight, which was the very latest he could arrive. He found himself unable to pass on the thruway and had to travel at a slower-than-normal pace. He decided not to look at his clock the entire distance.

> After leaving the thruway everything went wrong. A car pulled out in front of me going two miles per hour. At that time I had a different feeling--almost like serenity--giving up. I had it real clear in my head that we would be there at ten of eight. Cars would come and go. I didn't know how or what will happen. I could just sit back. Soon that car disappeared. A logging truck pulled out in front of me but I wasn't anxious. I didn't panic or try to pass because I just <u>knew</u> I would be there at ten of eight. I spent a longer time at the main intersection in town. Based on my previous experience, the whole trip would

have taken a little over one hour. We didn't look at the clock or have the radio on the whole way.

I pulled into the parking lot and it was exactly ten of eight. It was not nine of eight or eleven of eight. It was ten of eight <u>just as we knew it would be.</u> It was an incredible experience. I have driven this many times and I know how long this takes. On the one hand, I was surprised. But on the other, I wasn't. It wasn't logic. It was just <u>knowing.</u>

Notice the reference to "giving up" and trusting that he would arrive on time regardless of the delays he was experiencing. As he said at the conclusion of this statement, this could not be explained by logic. He simply trusted in the outcome, "knowing" that he would arrive at the desired time.

Belief about time can manifest very simply. One manifestor was talking to a banker and casually asked him when he got to work. Without hesitation, the banker said, "Seven twenty-six." The manifestor remarked that that was a rather odd time to begin work. "That is not the time I start work," the banker replied, "that is the time I always arrive at work." He added, "It doesn't seem to matter when I leave my home. But I notice I <u>always</u> get here at seven twenty-six."

The power of habit and belief is illustrated in this little example. Although not familiar with our concept of manifestation, he was still practicing this principle. He simply "knew" he would always arrive at 7:26 and he did!

Mind Over Matter

Can thoughts affect matter? I remember before I became very involved in this project lying on the beach and demanifesting clouds. I never picked a very large cloud because I knew my own disbelief system would get in the way of this demanifestation. I would choose a small cloud and focus my attention on it. Then I would close my eyes and visualize it becoming thinner and thinner and wisps of it sheering off and spreading in all directions. I would open my eyes and see it smaller than it was before and then repeat the process until it totally disappeared. I did this many times and almost always successfully. When it didn't work I recognized that my ego was involved. Perhaps I had told someone I could do it or I worried what would happen if it didn't work. Once I manifested a small cloud where I had previously demanifested a cloud. For some reason I never tried it again.

On another occasion, I also had a feeling--nothing I could prove--that at an outdoor concert a large group of us held off a predicted shower until the conclusion of the concert. The rain began a few minutes after the performance as we were all returning to our cars.

One member of the group related a similar incident at a different concert. "It started as a mild drizzle and what went through my mind and maybe others' minds was, 'I hope it stops.' And it did! Coincidence many would say, but as soon as the concert was over, it began to come down hard, as if everyone let go of the 'Don't rain' thought together."

But could we alter mechanical things, solid objects, simply by using our minds? I had read of a famous study by Robert Jahn and Brenda Dunne from Princeton's engineering department, in which a group of volunteers sitting in front of a random number generator could influence the number of 0s and 1s simply by desiring it. We also had a member of our group who could somehow use her mind to "soften" the molecules of a spoon handle so it would bend like a piece of warm licorice.

Another manifestor had to use liquid plumber to clean out a clogged bathroom sink. Unfortunately a small leak appeared in the plastic pipe, and he was about to call a plumber when he thought of visualizing a repair. After all, it was only a small leak.

> My bathtub faucet had a steady drip to it. I decided to try to stop the drip with my intent. I simply sent out to the faucet the desire it would stop dripping with very little effort several times a week. I would also visualize a substance plugging the leak. For several months it would stop for a few days and then start again. Eventually it stopped permanently, although I could not pin down the exact time this happened

because I had kind of given up on it. Maybe it would have happened anyway. Maybe.

Earlier we told the story of the broken ejector on the car tape player and how two group members were determined to manifest a "miraculous" repair through the strength of their combined visualizations. Their attachment to a fixed outcome probably slowed it down, but one day it was fixed quite effortlessly by a passenger riding in the car who "coincidentally" had his tool kit with him.

This incident was stimulated by the repair of a car radio. The manifestor did a lot of traveling as part of her job, driving eighty to one hundred miles each day, and she loved listening to her radio. She had been having increasing problems with her radio for over a year and had brought it to a repair shop several times. Each time they removed it and worked on it. Finally they told her she needed a new radio, to the tune of $160.

> I had sort of given up on the radio in the car and was fantasizing on what a neat thing it would be if we humans really could manifest repairs of our many material appliances. We might not have such a solid waste problem. I got the idea that if I meditated on the vibrations around the radio I could fix it. I tried to change the vibrations around it and went at it mentally with firm intent. I thought it was a lark, but why not? I'd have fun with it, anyway. Well, the day after, the radio came on. But then it conked out. So I thought, why not try again? It happened

about 15 to 20 minutes after I started meditating. I did this several more times and then it stayed on. I had to believe it would work. I really believe I have repaired my radio with my mind! Wow! I could put the radio repair folks out of business.

It is interesting that she was successful when she had "given up on the radio" and thought she would "have fun with it anyway." It took several meditations to create a "permanent" repair. As she remarked, "I had to believe it would work." The radio repair manifestation inspired another member of the group:

After the meeting, I thought about my radio, which hasn't worked in over a year. I raced upstairs to my old bedroom and darned if that radio didn't come on loud and clear. The radio itself works and I couldn't believe it. I told my mom, who had been having trouble with her radio, and she said that her radio had begun working, too.

Like the "flexible time" experiment, where one manifestor told the receptionist of his experience and she in turn told her son, there is something exciting about breaking through the limitations of former beliefs. Once one of us had done something, it seemed quite possible for the rest of us to do it. We were constantly learning how self-imposed all our limitations of what we could do really were.

Several group members found car repairs a fruitful area for manifesting. One was caught in heavy traffic and her car's engine temperature began to rise rapidly. She began "visualizing white light coming down through me and surrounding the car and moving out to other cars. The temperature dial of my car moved steadily downward below the halfway point, where it stayed." Another member wrote that her seat belt did not work and she "did not want to spend $200 to get it fixed." She did not work very hard on manifesting a repair, though, illustrating the importance of effortlessness and detachment as conditions of successful manifesting.

> I said, "Wouldn't it be nice if it healed itself? If it doesn't, I'll get it fixed when I can afford it." I didn't say it very often. I didn't have much attachment to whether it worked or not. I gave it up to the universe.

One morning, while getting into her car, she noticed the seat belt was working again.

One member, who was strapped for money and had to get her car through inspection, had a faulty engine that she could not afford to repair. The mechanic had warned her of a "rod that blows through the piston and then goes through the engine and then the car is done for." She knew little about cars but visualized as best she could the interior of the engine.

I did it with my huge planetary healing wand and I programmed the crystal in the car. Every time I get in I'm healing her. Well, after the first day, the noise went away and I haven't heard it since. How's that for some manifestation?

Needless to say, the mechanics were amazed when she brought it in again and the car was able to pass inspection. A year later the same mechanic still remembered the incident and told another member of the group, "We had a client who fixed her car with crystals. We had told her it was way too far gone. I can't explain it." She sold the car soon after and a year later it was still running for the new owner.

One group member had inherited a rototiller from his mother-in-law's estate. The tiller worked fine at first but then the gear box froze up. He and his brother-in-law (who is mechanically inclined and fixes computers by profession) examined it and realized the whole gear box would have to be replaced. Instead of paying a major repair bill, he decided to manifest a repair even though this went against his conventional beliefs. His personal account is instructive because he had to deal with his own resistance to a new set of beliefs.

At first I was reluctant to try. After all, I would feel pretty dumb if it didn't work. I mean I saw the gears and my whole life experience as an engineer said it could not be fixed without major mechanical work. I did know of examples where people fixed radios this way (from the manifestation group). When I sat with this apparent problem, I realized I had a lot of support for my conventional beliefs, but only a few second-hand accounts for mechanical repairs using manifesting. I knew that your beliefs affected manifesting and I seemed to be faced with the problem of throwing out my old, well-supported beliefs and embracing new beliefs, a process that I was sure would take a lot of energy.

Not liking this choice, I decided not to change my beliefs. After all, they have served me well. Instead, I just put them aside and allowed an opening for other possibilities. With this in mind, I approached this repair as an experiment.

I started to use visualization. At first I had trouble focusing my energy and getting a clear image. When I paid attention to the little voice in my head, I realized I had a problem with when it would be fixed. Fixing it instantly was too big an opening for my beliefs and the little voice in my head was coming in with many doubting messages. When I gave the process three weeks I was able to quiet this voice. At this point I had a clear image of myself using the tiller in the garden and it was working just fine. When I reached this point I just let go and trusted the universe would take care of the details. I felt good. I was not invested in the results. I just knew that what ever happened that it would be okay.

I did not give this another thought until about five weeks later, when I came across my tiller while I was cleaning out the barn. So I started it up to see if it worked. It worked just fine. I was very surprised to find that I was not surprised when it worked. Then my logic kicked in. In some way I had to make sense out of all this. The only way I could do this was to classify this as a fluke. At the same time this internal dialogue was going on, there was another part of me observing this chatter. I noticed how hard I was trying to take this experience and fit it into my present belief system. At the end I dropped the logic, accepted the experience as such, and gave thanks that my tiller was fixed.

For many of us, taught to only trust a certain set of beliefs lodged in Newtonian principles of the solidity of matter, to accept the power of mind to fix mechanical objects is extremely challenging. Note that this person did not give up his beliefs. He simply put them aside temporarily and treated this situation as an experiment. He knew the limits and boundaries of his beliefs, and he accepted where he was at the time. Thus he did not set an "unreasonable" time limit for the repair to manifest. He released the result "to the universe" and detached from the outcome. He actually forgot about it.

Some set of circumstances led him to the barn some five weeks later to discover that the manifestation had been completed. Even then, he had to struggle with the desire to appease his "alternate" belief system by attributing the result to a "fluke" occurrence.

In concluding this chapter, it is interesting to raise the question we presented at the outset of this section: Are there any limits to what we can manifest? We have found none--save the limits imposed by our own imaginations and the limits we accept for ourselves of what we have been taught is impossible. We know of numerous documented cases where people have walked unharmed on burning coals. No one, on the other hand, has walked on water, although we all know of one religious figure who reportedly did so.

It is undoubtedly possible to walk on water, but to truly believe it possible is a huge leap of faith for our belief systems. None of us has actually done this in his or her own lifetime, so we have no experience on which to draw. Nor do we know of others who are presently able to walk on water. At least not yet.

And limits, of course, have their value. There is comfort and security in the predictable; it can be frightening to go beyond what we believe is normal and possible. If you want to do so, we suggest working with your present belief system, wherever it is at the moment. Accept that all your chosen beliefs about limitation are fine. Such self-acceptance gives you an opening for change.

If using your mental power to fix a car engine is too challenging to your belief system, then repair a small leak in a pipe or perhaps encourage a cassette recorder with some minor deficiency to perform more efficiently. If you need to be able to allow for the possibility that it fixed itself without your conscious intervention, then work with that belief. Perhaps the leaky pipe in the bathroom just happened to have a plug of toothpaste solidify over the small hole. If your belief system requires rational understanding, then respect it, give it some information, and try to "stretch" the belief a little further the next time.

Be gentle with yourself. You are beginning to create an entirely new way of looking at the world around you.

CHAPTER 8

TRANSFORMING OUR PERCEPTIONS

As our group practiced manifestation for several months, we noticed a change in our perceptions. We became more aware of the link between internal beliefs and external events. We were more likely to look into our thoughts, wishes, and feelings when our experiences seemed puzzling. In other words, we began to accept responsibility for what was unfolding in our lives. We also enjoyed a greater appreciation of the way experiences and events presented themselves from moment to moment. We found that the flow of our experiences had greater meaning and significance.

A broader change in perception also occurred, at which we have so far only hinted. This change was an increasing awareness that we could view all of life as a series of learning opportunities. Even when we appeared to be experiencing frustration and hardship, we found that we could look on such experiences as challenges and even as opportunities for growth and happiness. We realized, as we took more responsibility, that we were never victims. Even apparent adversity brought further opportunities for growth, and we found ourselves achieving our desired goals in ways we could never have anticipated.

Discovering and Changing Root Beliefs

When most of us began manifesting, we chose some very specific and manageable goals where we could receive immediate and verifiable feedback. This was important for us because of our initial skepticism, and it helped us to build more trust in our own powers to create our reality. The process was very conscious and concrete. A parking spot was a good starting place. It was something almost all of us needed to create frequently, it allowed us to practice detachment, and it was immediately verifiable. Other early goals included articles of clothing, small personal items, and experiences of convenience in going through daily life.

Most of us wanted to see, however, if we could create more meaningful experiences, if we could manifest larger, more complex goals that were more challenging. Often we had to reverse the manifesting process: we looked at what we actually created in physical reality and then looked for the belief pattern that had created it. If we were creating everything in our lives, then we wanted to understand the origin of all our particular creations--even those that at first appeared not to be of our choosing.

If we consciously wanted more money or more time in our lives but instead found ourselves with less, some underlying or subconscious belief must be sabotaging our creative process. Like detectives, we ferreted out our obstructive beliefs. Was there a deeply felt belief in scarcity? A feeling of personal unworthiness? Guilt about living an abundant lifestyle? Any of these might block our desires.

Nor was it enough simply to identify the inhibiting belief. We also had to recognize how we fed energy to it, which might create even more scarcity. As manifestors, we needed to be aware of where we put our energy and then learn how to change that process.

Suppose, for example, that a woman made an investment that lost money. She could respond to this experience by concluding that she was not good at handling money which, in turn, might confirm an original root belief in scarcity. Her response to this experience might also manifest future scarcity. She might find it more and more difficult to escape the ever-deepening cycle and replace it with a belief in her own prosperity.

To make a change of this kind usually requires considerable practice and perseverance because of the often deep-seated nature of this habit. Imaginative little tricks can help, such as pretending one has sufficient income by making a donation to a favorite charity. Being open to receiving abundance in whatever form it comes, rather than being attached to a particular outcome, can also prove fruitful. Winning the lottery is only one way to attract money.

One's attitude, it has been said, determines one's altitude. By learning from the "bad" investment, for example, the manifestor can open the door to a better investment. She might choose investments that intuitively "feel right," even if they are not completely logical, trusting that they will lead to her desired outcome of abundance.

Our group found that if we expected to be successful and prepared ourselves to receive abundance, it did present itself to us. When we focused on failure or being victims of circumstance, we sometimes overlooked opportunities that were in front of us. If one door closed, we found it helpful to look for another door that was opening.

We tended to work with deeply ingrained beliefs, especially in dealing with mechanical objects. The "machine" could be the human elbow, a car radio, or a rototiller. Our "root" belief was that only physical intervention could create the repair, yet we found many instances in which mind power also worked. Each manifestor confronted this root belief, put it aside temporarily, and then had to deal with it when it re-emerged. Such a belief was founded on years of societal teaching, and reinforcement. To move beyond it would also take time and practice.

In the last chapter, we described how one person had successfully manifested a repair for his rototiller. Several weeks after this initial success, he wondered if the rototiller would still work. Doubt crept in. He was afraid to try it again. What if it didn't work? Would that make him a failure? He hesitated to try it. Eventually, though he feared it would not work, he approached the rototiller again. Not too surprisingly, it did not work the second time. It was a perfect manifestation of his own "doubt" of his ability. Years of scientific training as an engineer and experience working and repairing machines had created very strong beliefs in a "material" solution.

Another manifestor discussed in the last chapter created a repair on her car. Had she manifested a repair on the rototiller, it would likely have been successful. She was not a scientist and wasn't even sure what a car engine looked like, much less how a rototiller worked. For her, it might have been much like manifesting hard-to-get tickets to a popular concert or the perfect dress to wear to her friend's wedding, a dress which also happened to be on sale.

We also saw that we can work <u>with</u> our traditional beliefs rather than struggling to replace them. When we are obsessed with overriding our traditional beliefs, we signal our fear that these beliefs can't be changed. This obsession actually gives energy to and strengthens the old belief. The key is to work with and release this root belief while at the same time developing trust and empowering a replacement belief. The person with the tennis elbow worked with a sports medicine doctor first; then he experimented with the suggestions the doctor gave him.

Sometimes after I have played I will experience some discomfort and doubt and, at such times, will not hesitate to use a mild pain killer or anti-inflammation medication. Other times I won't need or use any medication, even after playing very vigorously. I felt very confident that my body was capable of handling whatever healing was needed. I would ask it what it needed and it would tell me.

This combined approach was also illustrated in the last chapter with the manifestor who injured her neck in a car accident. She used a regular doctor along with her "powered-up" visualizations and "band of angels." Her healing was very rapid. A scientist could not be sure which method contributed to the healing, but from the subject's point of view it was the entire healing "package" that provided the successful outcome.

We suggest that the practicing manifestor consider manifestation to be a powerful <u>tool</u>. It need not substitute for any other firm belief you have. You are unlikely to change a root belief or an established habit "cold turkey." Instead, you can experiment with new beliefs and use them in conjunction with more traditional older beliefs. Be clear about what you want and then be open to how your goal or desire comes to you. Do not limit the universe to any one way of healing or repair.

The group participants learned a valuable lesson with the repair of the car tapedeck cassette ejector. There was nothing wrong with trying to manifest a "miracle" repair by using conscious mind-over-matter techniques. But the manifestor was limiting himself and was trying to "push the river," so to speak. His beliefs were still anchored in the laws of physical matter. His passenger just happened to have his tool kit with him and within ten minutes had it fixed--this after weeks of trying to force a "miracle" manifestation. He could have saved himself much effort and frustration with a general manifestation of a repair and let the universe decide how it would be carried out. As it turned out, the process of repair was consistent with his belief system in mechanical solid objects.

And, of course, manifestation is just one more tool for creating desired outcomes in your life. Experiment with it. Learn where it is most useful for you. Stretch your beliefs for the fun of it and see what is possible. Life does not have to be a struggle. It can be lived with less effort and more efficiency if we so choose.

Manifesting with Effortless Flow

When many of us in the group began manifesting, we were very deliberate, specific, and conscious about the entire experience. Gradually we became less deliberate and detailed in our creations. One person, after a year of manifesting all kinds of material objects, was even getting bored with her successes.

I didn't even think of recording the drapes as a manifestation. I want the big stuff! This is so mundane. This is just living. These things fall into place for us all. I want miracles. I want to be able to change the world. I want to change everybody and not just change the drapes to make a nice home for me and my family.

For other people it was not so much a need to move on to bigger miracles as a recognition that manifestation had become a part of their lives. As one manifestor said, "I don't do so much <u>active</u> manifesting now because it has become an integral part of my life and not a big deal. So it just happens, and I think I forget I was manifesting."

We discussed this process of manifesting as being "in the flow" of life. Our manifestors saw this as "things falling into place." There can be an effortless quality about all of life; events seem to unfold in some perfect manner. In the group, we became alert observers of our own lives, appreciating how beautifully events and experiences seemed to fit together. We recognized that we created the events, but the intent was much more subtle than some of our initial manifestations. Sometimes we only really remembered the intent after it had already manifested.

One manifestor was thinking of changing his doctor's appointment to a different date and for a shorter time. He did nothing about it except think that a different appointment was more appropriate to how he was feeling now than when he had made the initial appointment four months earlier.

Within a few days he received a call from the doctor's receptionist. Would he be interested in switching his time to a shorter session on a new date? Needless to say, the new date was convenient and it was for the shorter time he had desired.

Was this coincidence? Why did the receptionist call him? He had expressed to her no interest in changing the time and date. How did she know of his desire?

A group member, a schoolteacher, had written to the mother of a teenager who had vandalized a building, offering to help in any way she could. Although no formal meeting was planned, she began to "coincidentally" run into her.

> Twice since talking with her I have bumped into her at the fitness club and have had lovely chats with her around her son, her fears and frustrations, etc. The interesting part is that I had never seen her at the fitness club before, even though we have both been members for quite some time! Of course we were meant to see each other. The last time I saw her, I even parked next to her. It was in an area of the parking lot I don't normally use. But for some reason I drove to it on that day.

She had just a simple intent and never arranged a meeting, yet her desire to help and the mother's likely need for help drew them together. Why did they not recognize each other before this "need?" Why did she drive to a little-used area of the parking lot that day? She knew "we were meant to see each other."

With time and experience in manifesting we become more aware of the effortless perfection of life unfolding. One group member who had become very aware of the process wrote about buying a new car.

I had thought it would be nice to get a new car at some time in the future. I loved the car I had but it was beginning to rust after six years and the repair bills were mounting. The clutch was going and another major repair bill was looming. For the most part my desire for a new vehicle was a gentle intent. I was not putting much effort into manifesting that I can recall. When I did, it passed through my mind that I would get the same make and model but perhaps it would be red instead of tan. These were fleeting thoughts that passed through my mind while out riding, when I could feel the soft clutch. My car felt less and less comfortable and my desire to feel more secure in a car, whether this or another, increased.

One sunny Friday I had no obligations whatsoever. Yet I did feel the day would be productive in some manner. As I opened the daily newspaper my eyes were drawn to a large back-page ad for a big car sale. Usually I overlook this page, but I kept reading and saw the color make and model I had thought about being advertised as one of the sale cars. I decided to look. Nine hours later I had a brand new car fully paid for. The salesman was perfect for me and led me to buy what I really wanted instead of a cheap imitation of what I originally had in mind. Things I hadn't seriously considered significant suddenly made sense. It was more expensive and had more options than I had originally considered, but it was exactly what I really wanted and was perfect for my budget. I just happened to have obtained a sum of money that would easily cover the costs of the car. The car was emerald green instead of red. Yet I knew it was what I wanted. It looked so beautiful. It felt so comfortable. They even had trouble finding it on the lot, as if it had been put aside for me.

Sometimes we get in the way of "flow." The following example shows how one manifestor recognized this and decided to "ride the horse the direction it was going."

I remember once trying to find a parking place at a favorite beach for my 85-year-old mother and myself and getting increasingly frustrated as I drove round and round in circles at a packed parking lot with no luck. Just when I thought I had a place some teenager would cut in front of me. It was a school holiday. Finally, I admitted to myself that my mother and I were not supposed to be there. I let go of the anger and frustration. While driving back home, we noticed a favorite restaurant and decided to have lunch.

It was very busy, but we were immediately seated, had a delicious meal, and were able to watch some dolphins frolicking freely below us in the harbor, a rare event. As we were leaving, I noticed it had become overcast, the wind had picked up, and it was definitely not a beach day after all.

Another manifestor noted, "I think I'm seeing more and more why things happen as they do." She had planned an event for a sunny day that turned out to be rainy.

The rain could have been a disaster. But it led to some wonderful opportunities. The whole set of circumstances just flowed from one good opportunity to another. If it hadn't rained, I never would have gone today, and I'm sure I wouldn't have allowed enough time to do what we did. It would have been a very different scenario.

As we become more familiar with the manifestation process, we recognize more and more that we are manifesting all the time exactly what we need. Sometimes it is immediately apparent. Other times it may be difficult to understand why seemingly bad things happen to good people. Ultimately we begin to learn, as one manifestor put it, "Bad manifestations are good manifestations that take longer to recognize they are good."

Manifestations as Learning Experiences

The person who made the statement about so-called good and bad manifestations was being stalked by her former husband and was wondering why she had attracted to herself this fearsome experience. Because of this incident she had to ask herself questions about her own worthiness and her persistent role as a caretaker in a relationship. It also stimulated her to tell her story to a newspaper reporter who was writing an article on this phenomenon just as the state legislature was considering a bill to make such actions a crime. "It was very satisfying knowing I might help someone. I always knew something positive would come out of this experience."

Manifestors increasingly saw how all events in life had meaning attached to them. The manifestor with the tennis elbow was, on one level, trying to wean himself from his dependence on traditional medicine for relief. On another level, he was learning about why he had created this weakness in his elbow in the first place.

A major breakthrough to a more permanent "cure" came while co-coaching with my partner in preparation for a challenging match the following day. We both played very hard that evening against each other, trying to overcome each other's weaknesses, since we would be doubles partners the following morning. After we had finished playing, I was surprised that I experienced no discomfort in my elbow.

However, the next day, after playing three sets, I had great pain in my elbow again. Why was there such a different reaction on these two occasions, given that the intensity of play each time was comparable?

The one difference I could see was that in one case I was competing against an opponent and in the other case I was empowering my partner to improve her game. I wanted her to play at her best and she wanted the same for me. It became clear to me I was dealing with a longstanding issue of mine around having to prove my self-worth through being better than someone else at any task, athletic or academic. I had learned this need to excel and win in my childhood from my father, and trying to live up to his expectations was the source of much dissatisfaction throughout my life.

I changed my mode of playing to one of coaching other players and found it always worked. Even when I played competitively I worked on helping my opponent improve his or her game, even if it meant some decrease in my own ability to win. I realized I had created this discomfort in my elbow as a learning tool, and as I learned my "lesson," so to speak, the pain disappeared. When I didn't emphasize winning, I played better, flowed more, and overall enjoyed playing the game more. It was just more fun. A longstanding major goal of mine was to create more joy in my life, and this was one experience that was doing just that.

Several months later he was playing with his son and noticed considerable discomfort in his elbow that evening. Was the old problem returning? They had played very hard but he didn't feel he had been particularly competitive. Upon further reflection, he realized he had focused on his son's competitiveness.

> I really wanted him to improve his play so he would get a starting position on the school team. His school team had won the state championship for the past four years and I was worried he was not good enough to win a starting role. I had simply transferred my competitive desires from myself to my son.

Gail Devers, the 100-meter gold medalist in the 1992 Summer Olympics, had to overcome serious illness to compete in those games. She was once within two days of having her feet amputated. What is remarkable is how she perceived her "handicap."

> My mental preparation is faith in myself. I wouldn't wish Graves disease on anyone. But I'm thankful for going through it. It changed me. It made me stronger. After going through all this you think, "There's no obstacle I can't get over." I felt like I wanted this race more than anyone else.

Rather than feeling sorry for herself as a victim of some horrible disease, Devers saw it as something to strengthen her, as a learning experience. She was "thankful for going through it."

About uncomfortable or frustrating experiences in her life, one manifestor said, "Bumps for me are a way I motivate myself. If it gets too smooth and easy, I get lazy. So I find some way to screw it up and get back on track."

> If I keep on affirming when things go well, maybe I won't have to manifest the bumps I need to stay on track. I try to take responsibility for my life and learn from everything that happens. I always ask what I have to learn from this experience and why things happen that way. It is a constant evolving process. This is another thing the project has helped me understand and focus on.

"Bumps," as she calls them, are her teachers. They are her friends. They keep her on her learning path. There is no judgment that one experience is good and another bad. They are just experiences that she has created, and she always has full freedom to choose how to respond to them. She can choose to be a victim or to be a student, to learn from them and grow in understanding, or to ignore them and perhaps create even more dramatic "bumps" at some future time.

> The lessons have gotten harder. Yet how I learn and my actual learning process, I think, has speeded up. It has become more efficient. I'm

seeing more clearly my part in things and how my behavioral and thought patterns and belief systems work in my life.

Often, these learning opportunities can be part of a major long-term goal, such as a romantic relationship. One person achieved his goal and manifested his "dream" woman. He noted how his girlfriend "came about the way everyone said it would--when I wasn't looking." He also makes a pertinent observation about what happens after a long-sought-after goal has been achieved. There is always more learning to be done. There is always another goal when one has been achieved. "With our relationship's ups and downs, I realize I have attracted exactly what I need to bring up those issues that I need to work on for my own growth."

The following example concerns a long-desired romantic relationship of one of the group members. From it we see how life serves as our teacher and facilitates our obtaining what we really want. The member had previously had two major relationships. Each time, she had felt hurt and disappointed, but she had also learned something.

The most recent relationship, with a person who was a multimillionaire, could have seemed very attractive since she was barely supporting herself by cleaning other peoples' homes. What he wanted was a personal servant, someone to wait on him. The past came back to haunt her and demanded that she heal it. She was being asked to heal a longstanding perception of herself. This was a "test" she recognized she had brought to herself.

> The universe had wanted to give me something to stand up to. He is very strong and manipulative. In my previous relationships I gave up everything to support him. I would give my all asking for love in return. That was the great test I manifested for myself. He was a great teacher. But I hope never to have such a test again.

> Ultimately I had to rely on myself for my happiness and my completeness. Those periods would become less and less intense and frequent. Once in a while I get lonely for a partner, someone to put my arms around. I don't get lost in those feelings. It will happen when it's right. I've always got myself.

> Every relationship you get into there is something there for your growth. You are preparing yourself for the ultimate one. You are attracting someone with a personal flaw to help you meet your own challenges. I felt I had achieved this with this last relationship. I had gotten to the place where I could be alone and earn enough to support myself the rest of my life. If I don't have real love, I don't want a relationship.

Over several years she went in and out of relationships where she found herself attracting and mirroring what she was to learn about herself. She was finding the "personal flaw" within that would help her achieve the healthy relationship she sought without. But she would not attract the healthy relationship until she achieved her own health. Several times she attracted men who treated her as a servant, reflecting her own low self-esteem. Instead of being discouraged, however, she saw each relationship as a learning experience guiding her toward her goal of a strong, loving, healthy relationship.

During this time, she learned how to support herself and be alone with herself. She did not give up her goal, but neither did she settle for just any relationship, even if it meant giving up a man who had millions of dollars. After one last relationship, she knew she had "passed" her self-imposed "test" and was ready for a healthy relationship.

I met him July 19th at 9:20 in the evening. We met at a class reunion. I met him within ten minutes of being there. There was some connection going on immediately. He listened to me for ten minutes. He said, "You have said more from the heart than I have heard from this entire group in the last two and a half hours." It was a recognition. The second night I was sitting at a full table when he entered. Another person at my table asked him to sit with us and he squeezed next to me to make a seventh seat. We both believe this is divinely guided. This is the first class reunion we have been to in thirty years. We both had been divorced, came alone, and ended up sitting together. That night I knew this was it.

The fairy tale continued. They had grown up two blocks from each other, gone to the same high school, and yet never had met each other until now, some thirty years later. She had planned to go into a convent and didn't. He had gone to a seminary and left. Their backgrounds were French-Irish. They both loved many of the same things, including Irish music. She was a singer, and on their first date they ended up singing Irish and Broadway music together. A caring, loving, giving, spiritual person, he was, her ideal manifestation. They were married less than six months after they met and now live happily on the West Coast.

She does not regret the years that led up to this relationship, even with all their hardships and disappointments. She realizes the relationship came when it did because she was ready for it. "It is good it came last because if it had come earlier, I wouldn't have known who I was and what I wanted to do with my life," she says. "The process works!"

The process is that invisible force that guides us and supports us along a path of maximum learning, even though we often don't recognize it. Sometimes it is dramatic, demanding and almost harsh, but the intent is always to promote our growth and learning. The partners we attract mirror parts of ourselves that need healing. Our romantic manifestor wanted a very special loving relationship, but to attract another she first had to be that person herself. Otherwise, as she knows, she would not have been ready and perhaps would not have recognized those qualities she so appreciated.

Choosing Our Experiences

Manifestors increasingly saw how they attracted each experience in their lives by their own thoughts, most of which were unconscious. They looked at what experiences they were attracting to themselves to get clues into their thoughts. Unconscious thoughts are habits and serve very useful purposes. How many of us have left work and started driving home, have let our minds wander--perhaps thinking about all the things that needed to be done at home or were left undone at work--to find suddenly that we have arrived at our destination! Yet we had not had one conscious thought about the mechanics of driving the car home. We had been on automatic pilot.

The same thing happens with many of our experiences. We go on automatic pilot often when we choose how we are going to experience our lives. Our choices or reactions are not only habitual but are out of our awareness. Automatic pilot frees up our consciousness to do certain things, since we can't always be weighing and evaluating every decision we make, but it also limits our possibilities. We may never consider a different way to go home. We may never consider the possibility that a "bad" relationship is actually preparing us for a "good" relationship.

One manifestor played detective when he felt "depressed" or "blue" on cold, rainy days. He noticed that he would think, "What a depressing day." Through his manifesting, he knew that there was a connection between that thought and his mood. He had long associated a rainy day with sadness and boredom. Many past experiences contributed to this evaluation. He decided to experiment with his thoughts and see if he could change his outlook.

> Now on a rainy and cold day, I say to myself, "What a great day to do all those things that I didn't want to do on a nice day! I feel great and have lots of good energy." I found at first that this was hard to do because it wasn't how I felt. But I did it anyway. The next week provided me with lots of opportunity--it rained every day. By the end of the week, instead of climbing the walls, I was feeling great and even joyous! I hardly noticed the bad weather. Much to my surprise, it didn't seem to matter. It is so clear now. It wasn't the weather that was depressing but only my choosing to see it that way.

This person is now paying close attention to his thought pattern. He is not only noticing what is happening in his life, but what the voice is saying in his head. He later writes:

It then occurred to me, why wait to detect a message that I didn't like before replacing it? So I just started saying to myself any and all messages I wanted to hear. I would say things like: I have great energy; I am joyous; I am loving; I am prosperous; Life flows perfectly; and anything else that felt right at the time. I also found myself being more thankful for all that I had. I have been doing this for three weeks and the change in my life has been dramatic. At times I am uncomfortable with so much joy and excitement. I am not used to it.

We have a choice in how we react to life. It can be either a positive or a negative reaction. Whichever we choose, it will attract more of the same.

Love and Fear

We are constantly presented with opportunities to choose love over fear, to see ways to grow and expand or to contract and retreat into our fears. One of the greatest challenges is to learn how to love those who don't love or appreciate us back. Loving without expectation of anything in return is called unconditional love. To love on this level is a challenge not only for those involved in manifesting but perhaps for all of humanity.

We close with three illustrations of the transformative power of love, the most powerful force for change we know. The first involves a teacher of elementary school children. This project member had a particularly disruptive class, which she said was "trying her patience." She finally decided to change her own attitude instead of blaming them for the disruption.

> The kids would never settle down and I kept trying different ways to get their attention. I found I was apprehensive when they would walk into the room. I would think, "Oh, no, here they come." I came to realize that the only reason they were disrupting anything was because they didn't have any love in their lives. I felt myself opening up and flooding the room with love. I did an affirmation and said to myself, "They are great kids." I looked at them with unconditional love. I did this for a period of a month. Lo and behold, they settled down, and now they come in and sit down and work and are happy.

In the second and third examples, we have manifestors who could certainly have justified taking a unloving attitude toward the person who seemed to be causing them so much trouble. Instead, they turned their situations into affirmative learning experiences about the transformative power of love.

> My first husband, a lawyer, left me when I was pregnant with my fifth child. I had no money, no address, and no job. I was trying to find soda money to feed my kids. I never did get support. He had two kids by his paramour and then ran off with his secretary. He was never in touch with me or his children. I had a hard life, did anything I could to make money, and sent all my

kids through college. The youngest is in the Peace Corps. I'm proud of what I did. Three of my kids reached out to him but with minimal response. Lately I have learned his wife has left him and he is a ruined man. I felt bad for him. Deep down, he is a very good person. Over the last five to six months, I have been sending him love and light. I shine light on him. There has been a turn-around. He has joined an alcohol support program. He has started getting in touch with a daughter whose husband is addicted to pot. He has sent her money and a book about codependence. He never had done anything like this. He has gotten together with three of my kids and seems to be trying to make some sense of his fifty-nine years.

I was working in a small department with six people. I had a good background for the work I did and the manager "shined" on me. The manager hired a new fellow who was motivated to move up fast by making everyone else look bad. I was the prime target. He was a good street fighter. The way he attacked me was roundabout, and I even thought it was my imagination at first. I saw my options as painful. I couldn't play his game. I didn't want to put more energy into dissension or keep the same situation going as it was. I was feeling angry. The message came into my head to love my enemy. How would I do this? I'm not going to give him a big kiss and hug him. I decided to focus on things I could love about him rather than things I was angry at him for. He did have a good side to him. At first it was hard and it was just teeny little things. The more I focused on the good little things, the bigger they were in proportion to other things. It began to out balance the negative side. At that point I could begin to love him. I was just feeling it. As soon as I got to the point of loving him, all those other games he was doing stopped cold. They didn't happen any more. I was glad to see him when I bumped into him in the hall. I could feel it and sense it. He became my friend, although I didn't have it that I wanted to become a friend. It was a very powerful experience. I didn't spend any more time with him than before, but the negativity and dissension disappeared.

Each of these manifestors could have easily felt justified in reacting with anger to his or her situation. The schoolteacher could have blamed the parents for the unruly children. She could have resorted to much stricter discipline to obtain order in the classroom.

The divorced mother of five children had every reason to resent her former husband, who dumped her and left her penniless. Instead, she felt compassion, sent him loving energy and support, and helped the children get to know their father. We have no way of knowing whether her energy directly affected her former husband, but the outcome is promising. She herself has little doubt of the effect of her prayerful message.

Finally, we have a wonderful example of a situation most of us have found ourselves in at some point in our lives. The unhappy co-worker would have been justified in trying to even the score with his manipulative colleague. Instead he chose a loving response. Particularly helpful to us is the method he used, which we can apply to our own situations.

Almost everyone has qualities we choose to like or dislike. We always have the choice of which characteristics we wish to emphasize and to respond to. The more we come to appreciate someone, the more we will find to appreciate. If we choose to see fear, we will find that, also.

Do we choose to see the superficial, some external aspect, and then project all kinds of negative characteristics onto that person? If he is a Communist, he must be some kind of dangerous aggressor who wants to annihilate us. How quickly that has changed! Were the Russians really all that different before Glasnost? Perhaps, if we all could learn from these three examples, we could go a long way toward creating an earth of love, peace, and harmony. But why not begin with our families, our colleagues, our neighbors, and--most important--ourselves?

Certainly love is the most important and powerful manifestation of all.

CHAPTER 9

WHAT WE HAVE LEARNED

Why Beliefs Resist Change

When we first began researching the concept of manifestation, we thought we had discovered a fascinating tool that would enable people to create more of what they wanted in their lives and thus achieve a higher level of happiness. What emerged was a far richer and more complex picture of how consciousness and matter is connected.

We found two basic levels of questions. The first was how to discover what the relationship really <u>was</u> between thought and matter. The second, even more interesting, was <u>how conscious we wished to be</u> of this process. We said in an earlier chapter that we believe we are actually manifesting our beliefs and desires all the time, though this process may be largely subconscious. We have the choice to remain unaware of this relationship between our beliefs and our experiences--and perhaps live our lives perceiving ourselves as victims of external circumstances--or to become more conscious of the various ways we create our reality. The choice is always ours.

If we decide to become more conscious of the manifestation process, we can also choose among many methods to create our desires. There is no one right method or one set of rules that fits all manifestors. We must experiment for ourselves.

The practice of manifesting desires has far greater significance than simply materializing thought. The real value of manifestation is a <u>process</u> that will lead to new dimensions of self-discovery and understanding. Simply deciding what to manifest in life can often give us insight and understanding into what we value. The manifestor who thought the perfect job was one that did not inconvenience her family and paid a lot of money was disappointed when she actually got such a job. Only when she began to acknowledge her own worth and accept her desire for an intrinsically meaningful job did she begin to attract more satisfying offers of employment. Not surprisingly, given the many examples we have recorded and participated in ourselves, we have come to believe that we can and do create our experiences in life. At the same time, beside this personal belief in the process of manifestation, we sometimes find ourselves holding beliefs that contradict this principle. As individuals, we are not a homogeneous and consistent package of beliefs, even when we consider only those beliefs of which we are conscious. It is possible--and very human--to believe that you can heal a sore elbow or fix a faulty rototiller through conscious desire alone and also to retain doubts of such an ability.

That it may be easy to manifest some things does not mean it is easy to manifest other things. The group member who was able to fix her car without mechanical intervention has been frustrated for years in her inability to manifest a lasting romantic relationship.

Few of us come to these principles of manifestation without also bringing with us a lifetime of previous beliefs that emphasize limitation. Some individuals may be able to make major instantaneous changes in their beliefs, but most of us find ourselves confronting an internal edifice of limiting ideas.

We live in a culture that looks for solutions to personal problems in the expertise of outside authorities, particularly governmental and medical institutions. Socialized to seek outside answers for many years, we can develop personal belief systems that are remarkably resistant to change. At times we may find it easier to see ourselves as victims of outside circumstances, even if this view makes us dependent on an external authority. Such a belief becomes self-fulfilling. The more someone resists the concept that she creates her desired reality, the more it seems to her that she cannot do so.

There is something comforting and reassuring about the status quo, of course, even when someone's circumstances are miserable. There is an old saying: "Better the devil we know than the devil we don't." We mistrust the unknown, and we fear risking what we already have, however meager it might be. And our cultural heritage tells us not to trust our intuitive guidance. Unless we can be objectively and rationally certain that some act of ours will translate into a favorable experience, we hesitate to take the risk.

Most of us also have a strong need for validation from others. Acting on the belief that we are the creators of our reality is likely to make us unpopular in a culture that socializes us to dependency and disempowers our capacity to meet our personal needs. This is particularly true if the circumstances for which we assume responsibility are unpleasant, such as an accident, illness, or personal loss. The belief that we need external sources for healing and validation keeps us powerless. Yet this belief itself, however much we wish to go beyond it, can prove intractable. Beliefs are necessary for us to live. They provide structure, order, and direction in our daily activities. At the same time, our beliefs <u>filter</u> what we see. First, they tell us what to pay attention to. Second, once we are paying attention, they determine what our reaction should be.

Once we were visiting a home for retirees. The home was situated in a bird sanctuary and had a beautiful outdoor swimming pool. An older woman was swimming back and forth under the watchful eye of a beautiful, tall, white bird that was waiting to take a drink from the water. The swimmer stopped and remarked to us how beautiful and graceful the bird was. Alongside the pool was another elderly woman in a wheelchair who seemed very agitated.

Containing herself no longer, she told the woman swimming in the pool to chase the bird away because it might soil the water. As if sensing its unwelcome, the bird gulped briefly a few mouthfuls of water and flew off.

Here were two women who saw the same event. One saw a beautiful visitor and marveled at its presence. The other saw a dirty invader that might soil a body of water she herself was in no condition to use. Each woman brought her belief system about nature and love and beauty with her, and each saw the same experience with very different "eyes."

We always have a choice--we can become aware of our beliefs or we can continue to pretend they are inconsequential. In either case, they control the circumstances we bring to ourselves. By knowing what they are and how they operate, we gain the power to replace those beliefs and circumstances we dislike. We can choose to perceive life as full of fear and threat or we can choose to perceive it as filled with love, abundance, and beauty. Is it a beautiful bird or an intrusive creature? The choice is ours--what we choose to "see" is what we will actually find. As the manifestor in the previous chapter looked for things he liked in a colleague, he found it easier and easier to notice even more things to like about him.

If you are unsure what your beliefs--your attitudes--are, you can simply look at what you are manifesting and ask what beliefs might manifest those circumstances. Life is a wonderful mirror of our state of consciousness.

We can view even a negative circumstance as an opportunity for something new and more desirable to take its place. Remember the man in Chapter 1 who always manifested bad weather on his vacation? Later, his awareness of the belief causing that circumstance allowed him to change it. And the person who was unable to attend a concert because it was sold out? He chose not to blame himself or fate for his apparent misfortune. His acceptance in turn led him to discover another concert and to experience even greater pleasure.

You Do Not Have to Deny Present Beliefs to Embrace New Ones

Change can come in many ways and at different speeds. Some people make dramatic life changes following a major crisis, such as a life-threatening illness or a financial disaster. For the rest of us, "baby steps" can accomplish the same results, though perhaps less dramatically.

An important first step is to accept ourselves and our beliefs and doubts as we--and they--presently exist. This acceptance <u>allows</u> for change. Beliefs built up over a lifetime may have served you well. You don't have to invalidate them. And changing your beliefs can feel threatening, particularly if you try to make such changes all at once. In fact, it is important not to deny the presence of beliefs strengthened over the years. To deny them gives them even more power because you are demonstrating your attachment to them.

All beliefs are limiting to some extent, but some are less limiting than others. We have found it is perfectly acceptable to work simultaneously with beliefs that may seem inconsistent with each other. There is, in any case, no one perfect set of beliefs. It's a matter of what works for you.

When you accept yourself and your beliefs, as we have said, you create an opening for change. Then you can use a variety of techniques--affirmations, visualizations, and personal experiments--preferably with a dose of humor and detachment. Manifesting as a process seems to work best when it is fun and when you have little ego invested in the outcome.

A second "baby step" is to start small and work from small manifestations to larger ones. If you try to take too big a jump, such as healing a serious medical condition through conscious will, you may not really believe you can do it, and you will not. It is perfectly permissible--and perhaps better--to use old standard methods along with new methods. The person with the tennis elbow did not, all at once, cast aside traditional medical treatment. He gradually weaned himself from traditional methods. Nor did he feel he had personally failed if he had doubts on certain occasions and returned to regular medical techniques to relieve his pain.

We want to emphasize that your present beliefs about limitation are not and have not been incorrect. Even if you choose to grow beyond your present beliefs, it is important to recognize and respect your old beliefs; they got you to where you are now. Especially, do not judge yourself. You can have a belief in scarcity and simultaneously begin to allow a belief in prosperity to grow within you. It is a judgment that there is or was something wrong with scarcity, or with yourself for believing in scarcity. Accept your belief--and simultaneously create an opening for a new desired state of abundance.

Learning to Enjoy the Process

Like the members of the manifestation group, you can learn to become artists of your own lives. We learned to find joy in the manifestation process itself, and we became less attached to or consumed by the attainment of goals. In a sense, our goal became to learn about how the process of manifesting our desires worked.

Of course, there was great satisfaction when one of us actually did manifest that perfect parking place or article of clothing. But it was equally exciting to recognize ourselves as being in the process called "flow," when we always seemed to be at the right place at the right time.

We even marveled at the process when we were out of flow, like the driver who had no time to spare and "happened" to hit every red light and delay imaginable while rushing to do his errands. Goals provide direction, but when we make them the ends in themselves, struggle to reach them, and become attached to them, we can miss most of the pleasure in the manifesting process. Worse still, we are likely to find our goals themselves receding further into the distance.

So learn to enjoy the process itself. It can become wonderfully liberating. In manifesting, everything becomes a learning experience. Our group increasingly trusted that all experiences were leading us toward our chosen goals. We even looked upon our setbacks as mysterious steps toward the realization of a desired goal-- their value might become evident at some future time. How could the concert-goer know, for instance, that being turned away from one concert was preparing him and his guests to have even a more enjoyable experience at another concert? How could someone who was unable to find a beachside parking place, and who instead chose to go to a restaurant, know that a half hour later it would rain at the beach?

Remember that money, desired experiences, or relationships are the <u>byproducts</u> of the manifesting process. Attaining them will only lead to new desires and new goals. A person who always focuses on the end result will always be living in the future while missing the joy of the present.

Creating a Supportive Environment

As we were increasingly able to see how our thoughts were linked to the events and experiences unfolding in our lives, we were able to create supportive environments for our process. We became more aware of what we thought, of our environment, and of the types of negative and positive people around us. It became important to us to <u>create</u> environments that supported positive energies. For example, we watched and read fewer negative news stories. We spent less time with friends and colleagues who chose to focus on the more fearful side of life. We knew that being in negative environments would likely affect our thought processes and, as a consequence, our manifestations.

As we learned more about the power of individuals to manifest their desires, we occasionally speculated on what the world would be like if everyone practiced the manifestation process. What if everyone on the planet believed in the abundance of the universe and their own self-healing powers? What would this mean for the overburdened and poorly functioning welfare and medical systems in our country and in other parts of the world? If we all felt we could create what we needed for ourselves, how might this reduce the level of blame and conflict in families? In towns and cities? In our national government? The possibilities for creating layers of positive environments were tremendously exciting.

As we conclude this book, we return once more to the question we raised earlier: Are there any limits to what we are capable of manifesting? One part of us believes that there are no limits to what can be created. Another part of us is skeptical--will we ever get beyond the limitations of many of our pre-existing and deeply internalized beliefs?

At this point we have no answer. We ourselves are still affected by deeply entrenched and reinforced beliefs in our human limits. To be sure, the manifestation project has gradually "loosened" us up, as well as the members of the group. Our thoughts, and the beliefs that give those thoughts meaning and value, are a little more visible to us than they were when we began. We are less likely to assume that our thoughts and beliefs are all that we are. We have more freedom to direct our experiences and interpret the events in our lives than we had earlier.

An Invitation

There is much about manifesting that we do not yet understand. We invite you, the reader, to help us explore this question of limits with your own insights, experiments, and experiences. Share with us your results and how you obtained them.

What have you found is possible, impossible, or difficult to manifest? Why do you think this has been your experience? What were your resistances to changes in beliefs? How did you move beyond them? Did you find, as your successes were built in small steps, that you were able to trust even more in your own creative power? Did you simultaneously find old beliefs drifting away?

We will include your results in our future work and publications. In that way, your experiences will assist not only your own manifestation process but will also help others in theirs.

Together we can create, strengthen, and become part of a new consciousness of empowerment, self-healing, abundance, and love. This will make it easier for more and more people to become aware of the power of their thoughts and to transcend their own beliefs about dependence and limitation. We encourage each of you to become a participant in a collective goal to change existing belief systems so that all of us and those who follow us will find the miracles of today becoming the accepted creations of tomorrow.

At one time the four-minute mile was felt to be an impossible achievement for runners. This is no longer so. Are we now saying that the three minute mile is impossible? For how long? Perhaps, once we are willing to expand beyond our present self-imposed limitations, those experiences that we today regard as impossible or too fantastic to manifest will, in turn, become the actualized miracles of tomorrow.

The question will always remain whether there are limitations to what we can create, for there will always be new challenges for us. That is part of what makes this process so intriguing. The attainment of some ultimate goal of manifestation is not what creates our joy and excitement. Rather, it is the ongoing process of working through our limitations and continually surprising ourselves with our own powers of creativity that creates much happiness, fulfillment, and peace. But, as we said at the beginning of this book, don't take our word for it. Try it and see for yourself!

--END--